Integrity @ Work

Using the Integrity Process To Find Your Financial True North

Ralph G. Adamo, MSFS

Integrity Wealth Management

NEWPORT BEACH, CA

Ralph G. Adamo/Integrity Wealth Management
3991 MacArthur Blvd Suite 215
Newport Beach, CA/92660
www.integrityiwm.com

Book Layout © 2017 BookDesignTemplates.com

Integrity @ Work/ Ralph G. Adamo. -- 1st ed.
ISBN 979-8-9875234-1-4

To Jean A. Adamo (12/19/27 - 2/17/2022) my Mom, whom without any advanced formal education in this area embodied Integrity deep in her core as a practice of daily living, whether that be with family, friends or complete strangers. I think she would be proud of this message.

"Integrity is the essence of everything successful."

–R. BUCKMINSTER FULLER

Contents

Acknowledgements

I want to thank all of the professional teachers and trainers along with all of the business coaches I have had on this path of education and growth - for without them, I would have had little chance of succeeding in this career. Names like Bob Seltzer, Joe Naselli and Rod Vitty whom as supervisors, taught me so many elements of financial advising. Then names like Dan Sullivan, Duncan MacPherson, Bill Bachrach and Ken Unger/Tom Gau all served as tremendous business practice coaches for me. Their contributions have been integral to how we do business today. And, since our industry is so supportive of each other, there are many institutions and conferences that have built my foundational skillset even further – the *Financial Planning Association,* the *American College* and even the *Million Dollar Round Table.*

Great credit goes next to each of our clients who have allowed my team and I to service their sometimes unique and varied financial needs since the mid-1980s. I have learned so much from each client relationship both about financial acumen, as well as human interaction. There is no better training ground than working with and for clients in honing one's skills, especially when the clients are sharp, well-educated and successful.

Without my staff, I could do little to deliver on the promises made to each client daily. One is only as strong as his or her weakest link and I have been blessed to have strong links in terms of team members now and throughout the years. They are dedicated and loyal individuals – each exemplifying integrity as a core value. For IWM clients reading this book - you know exactly what I mean.

Above all, I owe a huge debt of gratitude to Ron Stevens, father of Nick Stevens whom many know as the talent agent to the Stars of Hollywood. It was Ron Stevens who helped me secure my first position in financial services under Bob Seltzer of Cohen & Seltzer referenced above. Ron's insight was what made everything that followed possible in this profession. God rest his soul.

Of course, the love I have for my two children - Savannah and Christian as well as their mom, Amy and my two parents, Jean and Anthony has made the ride so far worth every bit of the effort.

Foreward

Clients expect strong technical ability from their financial professional. They also expect that their professional possess positive qualities and intentions – especially when it comes to the client's unique needs, personal goals and risk tolerance. What they might not expect is that their financial professional has moved completely away from a transactional approach with a fixation on individual products, short-term performance and pricing, to a directional approach supported by solid people, a consistent practice and a panoramic process.

Having known and worked with Ralph Adamo for many years, it is clear that he has a mindset that is strategic and client-centered. For Ralph, being a financial professional is not a job – it's a calling. As a goals-based planner, he doesn't just care about his clients – he cares about what they care about as individuals. He realized long ago that he doesn't just manage money, he manages a business that creates a consistent client experience. He manages client relationships through all market conditions in a way that liberates them to live their life with anticipation rather than apprehension.

Additionally, Ralph has an X factor that is very unique. He relentlessly works on himself personally and professionally. As you would expect, he is a serious student when it comes to his core competency, but long ago, he also saw the need to adopt best practices so that nothing fell through the cracks in terms of client service. Winging it in any way is unacceptable to him. Furthermore, over time, he developed and refined a process that uncovered the unmet needs of prospective clients who were introduced to him. This process also ensured that he got out in front of the evolving needs of his existing clients through fluid and dynamic planning – especially in the aspect of continuity, succession and family investment legacy.

Navigating through the complexities of dynastic planning explains why he has so many 2nd and 3rd generation clients. It also explains why he is so incredibly referable.

Ralph is also an unrivaled advocate for his sector of the economy. He is leading the way in showing other financial professionals how to move away from any form of salesmanship and instead, embrace client stewardship fully and completely.

It is very gratifying to know Ralph, and it was an honor to contribute to his book in this small way. He personifies what it means to be a professional, and he is the embodiment of *Integrity @ Work*. This essential handbook will not only provide you with actionable insights – it will galvanize your appreciation for Ralph. It certainly did for me.

Duncan MacPherson
CEO, Pareto Systems

Preface

I t's been my experience that very few clients and individuals have had adequate opportunities to advance their insight into financial advice and the advisors and firms that provide that advice. Because of the limited experience most clients have with various/alternative advisors – maybe engaging with one or two throughout their financial lifetime, their understanding of the professional contrasts that distinguish one advisor from another is equally limited. Selecting an advisor with this type of insufficient information can turn out to be extremely costly over the long-term.

My hope in writing this book is to help with this very concern. I would like you to take from this book two things: a) what should be expected from comprehensive wealth management and b) how to look for and assess a comprehensive wealth management firm.

Too often, our industry is guilty of masquerading under the guise of wealth management and using the term more as a branding technique, rather than delivering on what it should actually represent. It is my belief that the impact of comprehensive wealth management is not solely defined by the activities of the advisor, but rather, it is distinguished by the synergistic integration of those activities for the good of the client. Many advisors can do all the things a wealth manager can, but when that work is done in isolation, it fails to integrate all the pieces of the puzzle into a full and complete financial picture.

I'd like this book to serve as your guide to comprehensive wealth management's best practices and what that looks like when delivered to you on your behalf. All too often, there is a chasm between what people expect from financial advisory firms and the services they actually receive. A 2021 study of wealthy investors conducted by the leading research firm, Spectrem Group further reinforced this existing disconnect as evidenced in the chart on the next page.

The Gap -
Services Expected vs. Services Received

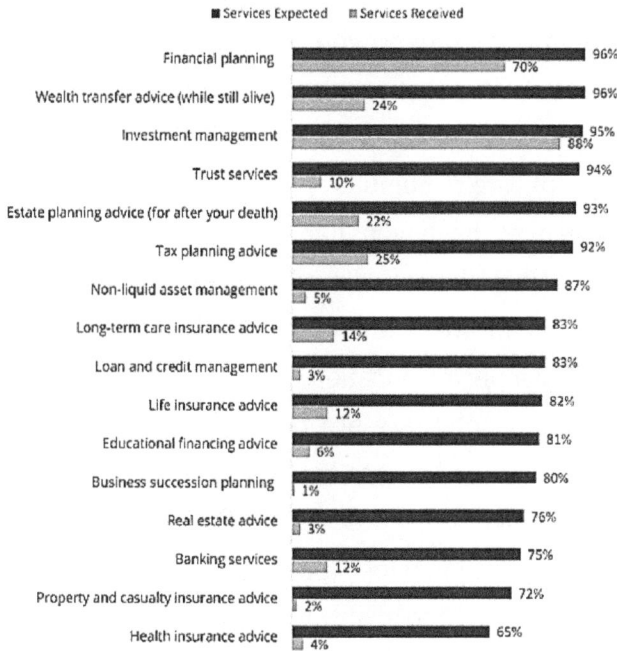

■ Services Expected   ■ Services Received

Service	Services Expected	Services Received
Financial planning	96%	70%
Wealth transfer advice (while still alive)	96%	24%
Investment management	95%	88%
Trust services	94%	10%
Estate planning advice (for after your death)	93%	22%
Tax planning advice	92%	25%
Non-liquid asset management	87%	5%
Long-term care insurance advice	83%	14%
Loan and credit management	83%	3%
Life insurance advice	82%	12%
Educational financing advice	81%	6%
Business succession planning	80%	1%
Real estate advice	76%	3%
Banking services	75%	12%
Property and casualty insurance advice	72%	2%
Health insurance advice	65%	4%

Fig 0.1
2021 Insurance Network For Fiduciary Advisors
https://in4fa.net/the-financial-services-gap-expected-vs-received/

Is your financial advisor meeting your expectations? Do you know how to compare financial advisors and the skillsets they bring to the table? By the end of this book, you should have your own checklist on what constitutes comprehensive wealth management in practice and recognize the skillset you require in a financial advisor.

Take the business owner selling a business. How many times in a lifetime do you think they are likely to sell a business? The answer is usually once. This is not applicable to business owners only. It's the same for many of life's pursuits and challenges. How many experiences have you had with filing a homeowners claim? What about finding that assisted living facility for mom or another family member? And, what about choosing a perfect location for that second home? More often than not these are one-off experiences with no playbook or road map to figuring out best practices. Most people when presented with these situations simply wing it. However, winging it or doing the "best you can" is far different than achieving a "best possible" outcome.

There's just no repeatability in one-offs and thus, there's little chance for mastery. The same is true when securing a financial advisor. There is no institutional memory or road map – no playbook for knowing what constitutes best practices or to even know what you're looking for when selecting a first or new advisor. Too many people rely on chemistry or a referral from a colleague or family member. This is a hit or miss proposition at best. Although they may have had a positive experience, chances are they don't know the financial terrain well enough to know all that should be on the table in terms of services, expertise and experience.

After decades as a financial advisor, I have learned that there are two things in life that can hurt us: *what we don't know* and *what we know that ain't so.* Getting the knowledge beforehand and being equipped with your own checklist on what to ask and look for is not just important, it is critical to your financial success. It improves your odds of securing true wealth management services and all the benefits that follow a comprehensive process.

The wealth management industry has matured. You no longer have to settle for less than a comprehensive and integrated approach to your finances. As you read this book, you should begin to see and understand all that is possible when you have the knowledge and the right financial advisor and firm helping you navigate to your financial dreams and goals.

P.S - If you're by chance a financial advisor yourself who's chosen to read this book, commit to holding the light of this text against your own processes and see if you meet or exceed the outline provided. All of our clients are better served when we compete in the arena of comprehensive wealth management's best practices.

This book is an outgrowth of our practice of always following the client's voice as our guide when charting their True North. Listening to your voice should be the unequivocal standard by which you judge every financial advisor and firm.

Introduction

in·teg·ri·ty

noun

1. the quality of being honest and having strong moral principles; moral uprightness.
2. the state of being whole and undivided.

Definitions from Oxford Languages

ntegrity – you either have it or you don't. It can be as solid as a rock, yet destroyed with a whisper. Some would argue that it's a dying virtue, a victim of our times and destined for extinction.

I prefer to think of it as Earl Nightingale did when he said, *"Integrity is the seed for achievement. It is the*

principle that never fails."[1] To me, integrity is much more than a simple virtue. It is a complete value
system – a foundation upon which everything else is built. Without it, little is sustainable.

To many, integrity and wealth management are considered mutually exclusive – an "odd couple" in modern times. That's not surprising when you consider the revenue-centric and firm-centric thinking that is so prevalent in the financial services industry today.

At Integrity Wealth Management, we like to think that we do things differently. It starts with our name, and we don't take it lightly. We hold integrity as a standard – we expect it of ourselves and what may be surprising is that we expect it of our clients as well.

We view this journey to your financial goals as a shared journey - a future that we share with you and a trajectory that we are on together. Our definition of integrity includes not only the traditional values of honesty and transparency, but also, the element of thorough and complete follow-through. Life is busy and it's becoming increasingly more difficult for many people

[1] [1]"Earl Nightingale Quotes," Inspirational Words of Wisdom, accessed December 19, 2021, https://www.wow4u.com/earl-nightingale2/#:~:text=Integrity%20is%20the%20seed%20for,the%20principle%20that%20never%20fails.&text=If%20a%20person%20is%20working,that%20individual%20is%20a%20success.

to get everything done. Our commitment to our integrity philosophy requires us to see things through to completion. If you don't arrive at your destination safely, neither do we.

Because we are on this shared journey with you - our client for the long-term - we look closely for clients who share our values. Many financial firms identify their ideal clients by simply establishing minimum asset levels. This actually translates into a pre-determined fee level required to merit the relationship. In other words, if you don't meet their minimums, they won't do business with you. We believe it is rather self-serving for a firm to declare such rhetoric even though it remains pervasive in the industry.

We define our ideal client as one with an asset complexity that warrants the level of sophistication our firm brings to the equation. More importantly, it is defined by a client's emphasis on what truly matters - sincerity to family and sincerity to finances. These elements result in a mutually beneficial and collaborative relationship between firm and client. However, what's more important to us when evaluating whether we are a good fit is a potential client's attitude and approach to life and to economics.

The people we work with tend to be a lot like us. They are optimistic, reasonable and transparent when it comes to their situation and their goals. They value close relationships and the trust that grows from such relationships over time.

I wrote this book for people who value integrity. We accept how important it is in life, but it's absolutely essential to your success in a relationship with any wealth management firm you choose to do business with - including the one you may be with now.

Typically, most people have fairly limited experience when it comes to financial advisors. You may have done business with your existing advisor for a handful of years or longer. However, a limited experience with different financial advisors can make it difficult to fully appreciate the substantial contrasts in services offered by different firms. This narrow scope of experience makes it hard to accurately gauge the quality of an advisor or understand the full capabilities of a true wealth management firm.

Many rely solely on the "chemistry factor" – this person seems nice, competent and trustworthy. Often, people are unaware of the full gamut of offerings and services available to them in a fully comprehensive wealth management program.

Remember, it's less about the errors of commission that should concern you (often they become glaringly obvious). It's the errors of omission that matter most - all the things that should have been there that were left out.

Throughout this book, I'll show you time and time again why integrity is so important and the role it plays in orchestrating your long-term success. I'll explain exactly how to look for it and how to recognize it in a wealth management firm. It's not just the powerful nature of the virtue alone that brings value to wealth management. What should also be present is the integral and integrated comprehensive elements that wealth management actually avails to you.

It's also my intention to pull back the curtain and show you how we build integrity into our systems, processes and the decisions we make for and with clients every day.

Working as a wealth advisor is not a job to me, nor is it a career. It's a lifestyle of helping people we care about navigate the many aspects and stages of their lives - financial and otherwise.

Something I've learned over the years is that we can't be all things to all people. Nor do we want to be. What we do want however, is to be all things in wealth management to a select group of people who share our values – people who are engaged and because of their engagement, can look to the future with anticipation rather than apprehension, as so many unfortunately, do experience. How big we get is not important. What's most important to us is how intimate we can remain with all of our client relationships under the forces of natural growth.

As you read through the book, take some time to reflect on the financial standards of integrity shared. Examine the standards you hold for the people you currently work with both within and outside of wealth management, as well as your own standards of integrity as a client and individual. Who in your professional and personal life is meeting, exceeding or failing to meet those expectations? I have found that scrutinizing this one aspect of our lives makes all the difference in profoundly positive ways.

This one skillset is one of the most important ones you can develop when moving forward in the direction of your financial goals and dreams. Reading the book in its entirety will provide you with a wealth of information to help you to take full advantage of the ideas presented. However, we all live busy lives that seem to get busier with each passing day. Another alternative would be to skip to Chapter 8 – *Roadmap Checklist to Financial True North*. This chapter pulls the most important concepts in the book together into a checklist that you can begin to use immediately. You can then utilize the rest of the book as a reference as needed.

Throughout this book you will continuously learn and develop a sharper lens for recognizing excellent vs. mediocre and great vs. acceptable with respect to everything wealth management. Moreover, you'll understand and appreciate just how much an advisory firm should be committed to your success - long before they strive for their own. You'll become equipped with the knowledge to separate fact from fiction - giving you the ability to chart a course aimed at True North— financially and emotionally in a clear and practical manner. After all, you deserve success on the many levels this journey called life should and can afford you.

Chapter 1

Ideal Advisor + Ideal Client = Ideal Relationship

"Synergy is better than your way or my way.
It's our way."

—Stephen Covey

How do you define value? What exactly does it mean to you and do you always recognize it? The term is subjective by its very nature and its interpretation can vary dramatically from one individual to another.

Within the context of wealth management advice, you may at first glance believe the value of a financial advisor and a wealth management firm is easily quantifiable. After all, you can gauge it by simply comparing performance figures over various time periods, correct?

That may be the case for some advisors because that's really all they bring to the table. They may or may not have done a financial plan for you - taking the time to understand your financial position and life objectives. They likely hold a portion of your investments and if you happen to be one of their top 50 clients, you may receive a call from them at some unspecified time which typically equates to only once or twice a year in many instances.

However, a true wealth advisor with a dedicated team and firm can and should mean much more to you than an annual performance number. We believe financial independence necessitates a holistic and panoramic view of your entire financial picture with all of its component parts synergistically working together. The old-school piecemeal approach to finances is ineffective and even obsolete – so is the old-school financial advisor trapped in that paradigm.

Covid is just the latest confirmation of how quickly world events, financial markets and life, itself can change. Our world is evolving at an almost exponential pace. Success is no longer a destination, it is a direction - one you must chart, navigate and adjust for, long-term. Finding your "True North" and continuing to move in that direction regardless of world, financial and life events is essential to navigation.

The Four T's - Time, Temperament, Training and Tools

Unless you possess in sufficient quantity what we refer to as the *Four "T's" – Time, Temperament, Training and Tools -* this is probably not a journey you should attempt or travel alone. You are unlikely to get the results you could or should achieve had you had the right team working with you and on your behalf.

Every household that has managed to accumulate some wealth should understand what power lies in delegating the technical details to professionals before attempting to fly solo. Not only are you likely to encounter substantial turbulence along the way - as all of us do - but you may find that life and circumstances can completely derail you rather quickly on your desired path to financial success.

There is a lesson to learn from the following quote. More importantly, the true story that follows is a near perfect personification of the quote's premise.

Bernard Baruch, American financier and advisor to U.S. Presidents Woodrow Wilson and Franklin D. Roosevelt once said, "I made (most of) my money by selling too soon."[2] Think about that...What's the opposite of selling too soon? Selling too late - and the consequences can be severe.

In early 2010, we had a prospective client arrive at our office with a referring CFO who formerly worked with Ernst & Young, the Big Four International Accounting Firm. This referring CFO was and still is a client of our firm and his hope was that we could do something to help his colleague correct his financial course. The prospective client shared how he'd gone from earning a significant 7-digit annual income from his private company, having a private jet and a substantial 8-digit net worth to now having to work for someone else and for a relatively modest salary.

---

[2]"How Selling Too Soon and Never Buying At The Bottom Might Actually Make Sense," Mercury News, January 18, 2018, https://www.mercurynews.com/2018/01/18/how-selling-too-soon-and-never-buying-at-the-bottom-might-actually-make-sense/.

The tale he told was as fascinating as it was disheartening. Like many American entrepreneurs, he'd built his company from the ground up. In 2007, he had an offer to sell. He couldn't seem to evaluate the full merits of the offer - its tax implications and how this would affect the lifestyle he and his wife had grown accustomed to over the previous decade. Furthermore, this prospective client was himself used to making all the financial decisions on his own. After all, who could blame him with the level of success he had achieved at that time?

The offer was beyond his wildest dreams of only a few years earlier. As you might imagine, he literally stressed out over whether to accept the offer. His apprehension had frozen him in place. He rationalized that his company would probably continue to grow and be worth significantly more, thus attracting an even higher bid in the future.

His income was strong and his lifestyle already enviable. However, his business as an asset was really all he'd saved or had to show for his efforts. Because the business grew quickly and most profits were reinvested to reach this pinnacle of success, he was left with little margin for error.

In a moment of vulnerability, he shared that selling his company actually terrified him for many reasons. The first and most predominant reason was one that often goes unexpressed by many business owners – a potential identity crisis. This is not uncommon when a business owner contemplates a future that no longer includes all the liberties, responsibilities and prestige that come with owning a successful business. A business owner who sells no longer has access to support staff who have catered to their almost every need and executed on their behalf day-in and day-out.

Another impediment we often find among business owners with an offer on the table is their limited knowledge of financial markets. They know exactly how to generate income from their business and have been doing so for decades. However, they are unsure of how exactly they can rely on capital markets to replace their earned income.

This prospective client also shared that he didn't have a solid advisory team in place that he could rely upon to sort through all of the tax, legal and legacy ramifications of a now specified sum of wealth. For him, it was easier not to confront the many unknowns associated with selling his business so he declined the offer.

Generally, business owners sell only once in their careers and as a result, they lack the necessary roadmap or playbook for selling a business strategically and seamlessly at an optimal price. Without a trusted team of professionals to help decipher facts and handle some of the softer emotional issues, many business owners don't sell at all or sell far too late.

The tremendous financial pressure resulting from the Great Recession of 2008 eventually caused his company's total collapse. Adding insult to injury, the situation proved far too much for this gentleman's spouse and family to bear, and when he came to see us, he was in the midst of a divorce. Money and the lack thereof, can expose relationship cracks and this was no exception. It's heartbreaking to think that this entire situation could have been avoided with the right expertise and guidance.

You have to have a solid fulcrum and barometer when it comes to balancing life and money, both individually and collectively. This requires four basic tenets which encompass the *Four T's*: *Time, Temperament, Training and Tools*. Either you have them in sufficient quantity or you don't. If you don't, then you must find the necessary resources to backfill for where you're in short(er) supply or you risk the consequences of poorly planned and even worse, poorly executed decisions around money and life.

Most people who are serious about building their wealth typically do not have the luxury of extra *time*. They are busy building their own businesses and careers. They consider their time more than a precious commodity and normally don't have extra to invest in fully assessing their financial situation. Nor do they have the time required to evaluate options of providers who could improve or refine their current circumstances.

Even if they can find the time, most admit that they lack the *temperament* and inclination to immerse themselves in the financial details required to discover viable and productive solutions with their current or alternative providers. In addition to that, they simply do not have the sufficient or current *training* necessary to understand all of the subtle aspects of their financial planning. Consequently, they may not fully appreciate how impactful some of their decisions and non-decisions could be to current and future generations. Without a systematic process for testing, measuring and verifying the nuances of a financial decision as it relates to cash flow, tax flow and ultimate net worth trajectory, you are clearly flying blind.

Tools such as financial planning software, financial calculators and even financial simulators are necessary to fully assess implications of the before and after effects of potential decisions. Purchasing and owning the software does not necessarily mean one is proficient in running scenarios and crunching data to arrive at the best or most informed financial decisions. I have yet to meet the client who owns or rents their own financial planning software.

Your advisor and their team behind the scene need to integrate the *Four T's* and become your virtual household CFO. There is power in delegating activities of analysis and review while retaining the authority of decision-making.

The surgeon should do as little of the pre-op and post-op as is truly essential. Consider yourself a surgeon with precious little time to perform all that is required to prepare and then subsequently execute on all that is necessary to implement. Build a team around you to enable and empower you in making good decisions. You must have a structured process and delegate the roles of *Testing, Measuring and Verifying* possible alternative decisions long before you decide on a any given one of them.

You either set your life up to have a trusted partner and team or you choose to do it yourself with what is likely less than proficient tools for discerning the good from the not so good. This is a critical step regardless of your brilliance in your own field.

Be aware of how the *Four T's: Time, Temperament, Training and Tools* present themselves in your specific situation. Are you taking proper advantage to leverage these elements in your financial planning as well as other aspects of life? Examine everything through this lens and you will make a quantum leap in generating better outcomes across all areas of finances and life.

The Ideal Financial Advisor

If financial success is your desired long-term direction as you progress through life, it's important that you are able to develop a long-term relationship with your advisor. We understand that placing your future in the hands of an advisor is not just a financial commitment but an emotional one as well. The best advisors understand that the most important bonds are the human bonds created.

It's important that you are a good fit with your financial advisor both financially and personally. The advisor/client relationship should have potential for developing into a close and well-connected one over time. After all, you'll be sharing your hopes, dreams, goals and challenges, as well as your family's future with your advisor.

On a personal level, your advisor should be a good listener and ask a lot of questions about you and your family. Conversations, plans and processes should all revolve around you – not the firm, not the advisor and especially, not the firm's revenue. A big part of an advisor's job is to educate, so you should feel comfortable enough to ask questions throughout the process. A good policy is to always understand at least on a basic level why you're doing what you're doing. We have found that clients who are informed actually make more confident clients because they understand the alternative paths forward.

Most advisors are likeable and personable people. Chances are you will like a lot of the advisors you interview, but avoid the temptation to choose an advisor based on chemistry alone. Your advisor will be your partner in success. It's important that you choose wisely by being aware of what matters most in the relationship. Although chemistry is important, it must be coupled with discernable competence if you hope to reach your financial goals. Many advisors rely on their relationship skills alone to maintain engagement with clients. We have found that this simply does not work long-term. It is inadequate for the work and sophistication required in the fully comprehensive planning process that business owners and professionals seek.

Now may be the time to peer through the lens of proficiency to honestly evaluate your current advisor's skillset and philosophy as well as the nature of your relationship. Are they meeting the standard that you desire for yourself and for your family's financial wealth building? (Refer to pages 70–71 for the landscape of Integrity Wealth Management's integrated concept of comprehensive wealth management.)

If not, start utilizing the filter of "what is possible" to find an advisor with a firm that can address the issues that are important to you and to your satisfaction. You no longer have to accept what has been "adequate."

There are many advisors who meet these elevated standards and more. Refrain from making your decision after just one interview. A former leader at a previous firm once gave me a pearl of wisdom that I've never forgotten. I remember him saying that once you've met one financial advisor - you've met one financial advisor. In other words, there is no template by which financial advisors are stamped out. You need to find the best available and by the time you finish this book you'll know exactly what to look for.

The Three P's – Philosophy, Planning Strategy, Process

As you progress through life, certain events are predictable – others are not. Your advisor should have the knowledge and expertise to anticipate and help you to navigate as seamlessly as possible through the many life events you will face. This can be anything from the arrival of a new child or grandchild, the purchase of a new or second home to the sale of a business. It can also be events such as death, divorce or disability. Each of these critical life events warrants a different response. Your advisor should be prepared and equipped to help you through these circumstances as easily as other key areas of financial planning.

In addition to being compatible on a personal level, it's also important that an advisor is capable of handling the expanding financial complexities that accompany increases in wealth. Outgrowing your advisor just as things are taking off for you isn't a good thing. The relationship should not be something you can outgrow, but rather something you grow into all along the way. We believe effective financial planning for your future is built on the sound and expansive concepts represented by the *Three P's – Philosophy, Planning Strategy* and *Process*.

At Integrity Wealth Management, we follow an *enlightened* philosophy that is central to our clients' financial independence. Because we're on a shared journey with you, putting clients first is part of our DNA. It's important to us that we integrate all aspects of your life - tax management, estate planning, debt management and risk management when establishing your financial picture. This helps us to create and maintain that panoramic view of your finances we spoke of earlier.

From this philosophy, we develop a *planning strategy.* Your planning strategy is unique to you. There is no one-size-fits-all when it comes to financial planning. It's important that we keep your financial journey fluid and dynamic with the ability to evolve as your life evolves.

Dwight D. Eisenhower once said, "...I have always found that plans are useless, but planning is indispensable."[3] We agree that financial planning is indispensable on this journey but having a plan with no process for execution is useless.

This is why we developed our proprietary planning process, The Wealth*Trac FORMula*™ which we will discuss in detail in subsequent chapters. The process integrates eight foundational pillars with the goal of taking all the pieces of your financial puzzle and putting them in place. Each plan and puzzle necessarily are unique.

The different pieces may not all be relevant to you or your plan at the present moment. However, as your life unfolds and your needs evolve, the Wealth*Trac FORMula* gives us a process that helps you pursue and maintain financial independence.

View everything through a comprehensive lens. Determine if your current advisor has a complete wealth management skillset and process, as well as a thorough

---

[3] "Dwight D Eisenhower Quotes," Oxford Reference, accessed 12/17/21, https://www.oxfordreference.com/view/10.1093/acref/9780191826719.0 01.0001/q-oro-ed4-00004005.

suite of wealth management resources to offer. Be honest with your assessment here. Few firms never mind, advisors hold themselves to a level of truly integrated advice. If you have one, keep that relationship close. It's unique. If not, it's time you source one that does fill these requirements.

The Ideal Client

We are constantly re-evaluating who we do this work for and who is an ideal client for the services our firm is equipped to deliver. You might wonder why we ask this of ourselves and not just think that anyone with money would be a good candidate.

After years of serving our clients, we have learned many things. Through experience, one of our most important lessons is that we cannot be all things to all people and deliver the level of service and commitment that we feel our clients deserve. Rather, our goal is to be all things to a select group of people. Through years of developing and refining our Wealth*Trac FORMula*, we have identified the clients that we are most suited to partner with and serve. We define those clients as those who possess the following *Three A's*.

Asset Complexity

We never establish minimum investable asset levels that potential clients must meet to do business with us. However, given that we see this journey as a shared and committed future with a high degree of involvement on both sides, we know that the client must have sufficient complexity in asset structure and size to effectively plan and grow measurably with us. We want to ensure that clients experience a solid value exchange when they engage with our firm.

Why such a nebulous definition of client asset structure and size, you ask? "Why not set a specific minimum asset hurdle that draws a distinct line in the sand regarding investable asset levels?" After all, the industry has clearly conditioned clients that this is the criteria by which one qualifies for a relationship with most firms.

When a firm outlines their criteria with a prominent declaration of, we have an investment minimum of $1 million, $5 million or $50 million - what are they really saying to you? This sort of statement translates into the firm's revenue-centric equation: how much are we going to be paid for taking on this client?

This can't possibly be sincere or genuine nor in your best interest. How can that rise to the level of fiduciary where the standard is about putting the client's best interest first? In my humble opinion, this does not even come close to meeting fiduciary standards, nor can it possibly put the client first.

Our mission is about *changing outcomes* positively and *impacting lives* affirmatively with the skills we have acquired and continue to refine every day. Next time you come across a firm that proudly advertises their investable asset minimums, examine their nomenclature and see how it sits with you.

You now have another lens through which to peer and examine true motives and thus, True North.

Attitude

We consider ourselves positive, realistic, respectful, grounded and fair-minded individuals. Maintaining our firm culture is important to us and as a result, we screen for similar attributes in our clients. Just as you want to find a good fit with your financial advisor, we want to find a good fit with the clients we serve because our commitment to our clients is long-term and highly personal in nature.

If our mission is to be *all things to a select group of people* with respect to their financial journey, we must be judicious in the relationships we engage in. It's not about how big we can become, it's about how intimate we can remain in each of our client relationships, while still growing the number of households we can positively impact.

As you read further in this book, you will begin to understand everything that can be done for you and how much of a partner the firm can become in your financial life. We are proud to say that our clients embody the same standards of integrity that we strive for in ourselves every day.

Our clients are generally friendly and optimistic people who appreciate our staff and our expertise. They value relationships based on mutual trust and believe in service to others. All of our clients are transparent and willing to share their complete financial picture. They are highly motivated to listen, engage and act on our professional recommendations, empowering us to do our best work for them. You too, should enjoy this level of transparency.

We feel there are only so many seats on our professional and proverbial bus and making room for a client who does not share our clients' values can disrupt the balance of the entire bus. This is especially true in light of the number of social and educational events we host for our client community throughout the year. Meaningful interaction is always the cornerstone of a relationship with Integrity Wealth Management and it should be with your chosen advisory firm, as well.

Advocacy

Our clients tend to be individuals who advocate and speak up for their friends, family and the causes they care about. They advocate for the non-profit endeavors that touch them and they make sure that those in their circle are getting the help and guidance they need.

You may wonder why this would be important to a financial advisory firm. For most firms, it probably wouldn't be - but for us, it tells us that these clients, like us, are trying to make a positive difference in the world.

These are people who care about others and are trying to improve their lives and the lives of those around them.

Peering through the lens of the *Three As: Asset Complexity, Attitude* and *Advocacy* are you enjoying a true partnership with your current advisor? Can you course-correct with your advisor on this partnering philosophy? Is he or she a good practitioner and a good human being, or should you consider looking elsewhere to deepen the relationship and likely improve outcomes?

If you don't get a sense of being on a shared financial path together - one where your best interests are always at the forefront of the planning, then it may be time to re-evaluate what you're doing and who you're doing it with. Being committed to a like-minded approach is imperative to achieving the best outcomes. Your financial and emotional True North is obtainable if you have the right team around you.

Chapter 2

FORM and Return on Life

"Family is not an important thing. It is everything."
— Michael. J. Fox

We live in a very different world today – one dominated by rapid change. It's not the same world that our grandparents or even parents grew up in or operated from when accumulating wealth. Gone are the days when individuals remained at the same company for 40 years or worked for a large company, then retired with a sizable pension, collected

Social Security and as long as they lived reasonably - were in no danger of outliving their money. In that world, where life expectancy was nowhere near today's expectations, retirement savings only had to last 10 or 15 years.

Fast-forward to today's world where you can expect to spend two to three decades in retirement. According to recent research, a couple aged 65 has nearly a 50/50 chance that one of the two will survive to age 95.[4] That's a full 30 years of retirement. As longevity continues to increase, it's quite possible that you may spend as much time in retirement as you did in your working years. When you compound that with astronomical health care costs, rapidly rising education costs and an expanding inflationary environment, it's easy to see why you need a solid and knowledgeable team behind you helping you navigate to your life goals.

As you progress through life, you will encounter many opportunities, challenges and events – some you'll have control over – others you will not. Our panoramic approach to wealth management is deeply rooted in *what matters most to our clients.* We focus on identifying

---

[4] "Life Expectancy for Couples: Why It's Surprisingly Long and What You Should Do About It," Monevator, May 29, 2019, https://monevator.com/life-expectancy-for-couples/.

and leveraging the *factors that we can control* and we operate in the space where the two intersect. Our Wealth*Trac FORMula* is the process we use to do that and we'll discuss it in detail in this chapter.

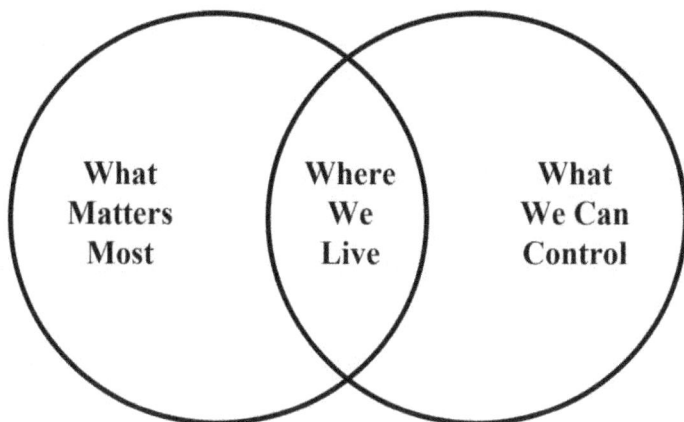

```
     What              Where              What
   Matters              We              We Can
     Most               Live             Control
```

The *FORM* in *FORMula* is capitalized for a reason. What's most important to you is the foundation upon which everything we do is built. We have found over the years that *FORM – Family, Occupation, Recreation and Money* encompasses the factors that are most important to our clients.

Family

Successive generations woven together create the tapestry of family. We designed our process with family in mind - a wholesome and thoughtful strategy that supports each member of the family at every age.

For parents, it's critical that your children and grandchildren understand where your wealth came from, how you worked to grow it and what you want it to accomplish for them after you're gone. We have deep conversations with you and ask many questions because it's not just about passing on *valuables* that is important in transfer planning; it's about passing on the *value systems* that have served you well in building your wealth.

In our family wealth succession planning, we work to integrate that value system so that subsequent generations have a compass with which to navigate *True North* and help steer their futures in a direction that's congruent with the legacy that was left to them. Whether it's the dynamic between parents and children or between spouses, our practices in this area are aimed at strengthening the bonds between family and across generations.

Occupation

Most people spend a large part of their day in or around their occupation. As we shared in a previous chapter, for many, their identity is closely tied to and in some cases, even dependent upon what they do for a living.

By working through our process, we give clients clarity on what exactly they desire from their occupation beyond merely income. For some, it may be planning for a work-optional lifestyle and for others, it may be creating a plan for a secure retirement at a specific age.

Regardless of which camp you fall into, our work with your occupation ensures that you are utilizing and maximizing every employment resource available to reach your ultimate goals. I can't emphasize this enough - our work is always built around you and what's most important to you.

We help you to fully prepare for voluntary employment transitions such as retirement or adjusting to a work-optional lifestyle. We also work to ensure that you're ready for unpredictable events like an involuntary closure, a disability due to health issues or even an untimely death. There is often a lot of emotion tied to one's occupation so our goal is to ensure that you are adequately prepared financially, regardless of what you may encounter.

Recreation

Our involvement around recreation is about enabling you to do more of the things you love to do both prior to retirement, as well as during your retirement. We want to know exactly what's on your *special bucket list* so we can plan accordingly. Because time really does fly, we want to help ensure that you're actually checking off some of those bucket list items throughout your life. I send my retiring clients a book by Ernie J. Zelinski, How to Retire Happy, Wild and Free. It helps focus the lens on just how rewarding retirement can be. In fact, a long time colleague and author, Steve Mueller calls it a time of *Reinspiration*.

We each have an R.O.L. (Return on Living) Quotient. It's important to plan for the *future* but, we feel deeply that it's equally important for you to have the resources available to spend more time doing what you love to do *now*. With proper and consistent planning throughout your life, you should be able to simultaneously enjoy your present while accumulating wealth for your future.

Just as there are life stages, there are stages within retirement as well. The first stage of retirement is your "Go-Go" stage. This is shortly after you retire when you have the time to do the things you've always dreamed of doing but were unable to do previously because of other obligations. This is the time when most retirees do a lot of traveling and exploring. You're still young enough to enjoy everything and still have the energy to do it. We want to ensure that this time in your retirement is truly golden.

The next stage of retirement is the "Slow-Go" stage. This is when retirees tend to remain a little closer to home and are generally more focused on home and family. This still encompasses recreation and fun but usually involves more time with children and grandchildren. The bond between grandparents and grandchildren is a special one in life and we consider this an important recreational component in your retirement.

The final stage of retirement is usually dictated by quality of health. Although not directly related to recreation, a little recreation can go a long way in preserving mental and physical well-being.

Money

Money can be the great facilitator and we consider it the vehicle that facilitates the other three components of *FORM*. In our planning process, we think of Family, Occupation and Recreation as your *"whys."* We view Money as your *"how."*

It's essential to us that we have a complete understanding of your "whys" before we ever begin to address your "how." It's one way we ensure that your money always fits your dreams and we believe this rises to a matter of integrity. It's one of the areas where we separate ourselves from industry standards. You see, these steps are typically reversed in the financial services industry. Many firms are more interested in the money component of the equation, while treating the "why" of the client as an afterthought at best.

Once a relationship with our firm is established, we view our role as one of stewardship and problem-solver.

We are vigilant in trying to anticipate and address potential hazards before they happen. We are also continuously tracking your changing needs and circumstances—regardless of whether those circumstances stem from external forces like tax and economic factors or from life events such as a birth, death or a change in marital status.

Each of these situations has obvious and less than obvious implications both financially and personally. You will often hear us say that the type of financial planning we do is less about the plan and much more about the ongoing planning, monitoring and review accompanying the plan.

Many times, changes in a client's life are seemingly innocent - like the buying of a second or even third home, the changing of a homeowner's insurance carrier, the refinancing of a property, etc. However, circumstances like these may require subtle course corrections upon examination of the finer points of this new arrangement. An interested advisor (and attuned staff) anticipates potential issues before they ever grow into problems.

FORM is the foundation of our Wealth*Trac FORMula*. It's how we process wealth management and see things through to completion. It gives us purposeful direction and allows all the pieces of your financial picture to work together and evolve as your life evolves. The Wealth*Trac* *FORMula* which we'll outline in-depth in the next chapter gives us structure yet provides the resiliency and flexibility essential to navigating a rapidly changing world. Peer through the lens of *FORM* in your current situation, using it as your beacon and guiding light to discovering your True North both financially and personally. Are you finding the *how* of money outweighing the critical *why* of Family, Occupation and Recreation in your discussions with your advisor? If so, much is being left out of the equation shorting you on what follows next...

ROL (Return on Life)

Our clients are important to us as individuals – not as statistics or as part of some pre-determined demographic group. We have a genuine interest in who you are, where you came from, where you hope to go and what's most meaningful to you. When we sit down to talk with you as our client, our questions are not just the standard superficial due diligence questions.

We know that everyone has a story, and your story is molded from your experiences. It's your unique personal history that builds your philosophy on family and money. Your experiences shape your value system, and your value system drives your decisions.

The better we understand you and what's really important to you on a deep level, the better we can help you navigate through the ups and downs you'll experience throughout your life. This means we listen on a deep level to gain the insight we need to deliver the highest level of personalized guidance and service possible.

We believe that it's important to balance ROI – Return on Investment - with ROL – Return on Life. Mitch Anthony, founder of the Life Planning Institute first introduced the concept of Return on Life in 2005 as a new and enlightened measure of success in wealth management. "As advisors, we are conditioned to make sure our clients have enough money," said Anthony, "But we really should be asking if they're getting the best life possible with the money they have."[5]

---

[5] "Repositioning Your Value From ROI to Return on Life," accessed January 14, 2022, https://www.mitchanthony.com/repositioning-your-value-from-roi-to-return-on-life.

This is precisely why we always begin with you and what the "best life possible" looks like to you personally. It doesn't make sense to begin with a financial plan and then try to work your life into it. We start with the life you envision for yourself and your family and then we build a financial plan around it to focus on and refine all along the way.

It's important that we have clarity on "your" definition of success so we can fully understand the impact your money has on every aspect of your life. Our Wealth*Trac* *FORMula* gives us the structure necessary to adjust and facilitate your life changes as they occur and use financial planning to create the life you envision.

- Who and what gives you the most joy?
- What are you excited about and would like to do more of?
- What specific role do you want to play in the futures of your children, grandchildren and even parents?
- What would you want to change in your current money management to align better with the life you dream of?
- What is your personal definition of success?

- What kind of legacy do you want to leave and why is that important to you?

These are just some of the questions we ask as we begin to shape a plan around you to keep the people and experiences that are most important to you at the forefront. Financial planning with integrity is much more than just rearranging investments and insurance around the circumstances of your life. It's about always keeping a holistic and long-term perspective on your values and goals.

When you consider baseline traditional financial planning, you probably think of things such as asset management, risk management, estate planning, tax planning, income planning, insurance and debt management. We all recognize these as essential components that work in tandem and are necessary for your financial well-being. However, in this traditional model, there is an underlying assumption that everyone is similar and the only unique variables are the numbers that are plugged into a calculation.

We all know that this is not reality. Those numbers are representative of a value system and quality of life that is different for everyone. The numbers exist to support the life you envision - not govern it. The concept of Return on Life no longer places exclusive emphasis on quantity when managing your assets, but rather puts quality of life centerstage. This gives you the peace of mind to navigate the many transitions you'll encounter over the course of your life.

Our team works to help you clarify and reach "your best life" in *every* stage of your life. Your values, philosophy and goals are always our guiding force in every aspect of planning that we do for you. This is why we refer to the work we do with clients as a *"shared future."* Both the client and advisor have significant stakes in the game and failure is not an option for either. Like the pilot says to her passengers, "If you don't arrive safe, we don't arrive safe."

We believe we earn our pay by helping you to separate fact from fiction, noise from signal and keep you moving toward your *True North* on your path to financial success - regardless of circumstances. Making as much money as possible is never the primary objective of a financial plan. Although we all love to see great performance, "beating the market" typically has very little impact on your day-to-day life or your Return on Life.

Looking through the lens of ROL – Return on Life – is your current situation focused on quality of life or just quantity of assets? Use the aperture of this lens to see more clearly how money serves you and not the reverse as can often be the case.

We view money as a vehicle for helping you arrive at the life of your dreams. Our Wealth*Trac FORMula* process which we'll discuss in the next chapter keeps you in the right lane.

Chapter 3

The Wealth*Trac* *FORMula*

"Change before you have to."

– Jack Welch

Today, most people would never consider driving from New York to Newport Beach, California without GPS – never mind expecting to arrive safely and on-time. The idea of navigating today's financial markets in our rapidly changing world without a planning strategy that is both fluid and dynamic has an even lower probability of success than driving across the country with no GPS! There is no financial sunrise or sunset to even begin to calibrate east vs west as you travel through this life.

We developed our proprietary process, the Wealth*Trac FORMula* to give our clients confidence, as well as provide steady and purposeful direction toward their financial goals, regardless of life events. This process, as stated earlier, allows us to take a panoramic perspective on financial planning. Financial plans become outdated sooner or later regardless of how precise they were at inception. However, financial planning all along the way is essential.

Our objective from the very beginning has always been to help individuals and families become successful in their lives in whatever way they choose to define success. Our Wealth*Trac FORMula*™ helps us to organize our clients' financial lives in a format that makes sense and is easily understood.

Developing and maintaining a close partnership with you is essential to an effective financial planning process. This arrangement keeps both you and us aware and informed of any new developments which could affect your plan in one or more strategic areas.

We view our role as one of stewardship in helping you achieve your financial and lifestyle goals. As such, and as part of our Wealth*Trac* FORM*ula*™ process, we believe it is our responsibility to perform the following on an ongoing and consistent basis:

- Acquire and maintain a thorough understanding of your financial goals
- Update your current financial information as your life unfolds and your needs evolve
- Carefully determine and monitor your investment risk and time horizon
- Explain the implications of all recommended financial planning strategies
- Update you as appropriate by appointment, email, mail and phone
- Meet with you regularly to review your personal financial situation
- Act as your primary financial advisor and co-steward of your financial future
- Coordinate with other professionals when your plan requires it
- Treat you with the utmost respect and professionalism

We take the many pieces of your financial plan and arrange them so they are cohesively working together for your benefit and protection. Each plan is unique and although all pieces may not be relevant to you or your plan currently, as your life unfolds and your needs evolve, the Wealth*Trac FORMula* gives us the structure and flexibility to evolve with you.

The Wealth*Trac FORMula* is a comprehensive strategy and is designed to be just that - comprehensive in nature. Within it, we integrate the following eight foundational pillars:

- ***Portfolio Management***
- ***Income Planning***
- ***Liability Analysis***
- ***Tax Awareness Planning***
- ***Risk Management***
- ***Estate and Legacy Planning***
- ***Philanthropy***
- ***Value-Added Services***

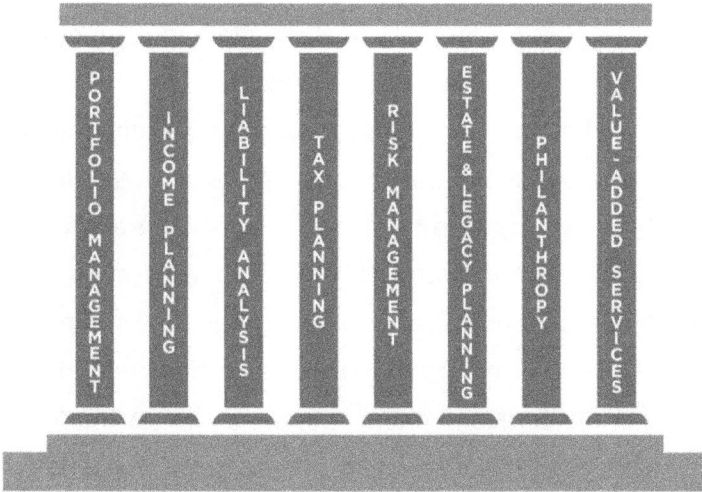

Pillar 1: Portfolio Management

When people think of a financial advisor, most believe the job description begins and ends with the first pillar listed - portfolio management. For many financial advisors, that is indeed the case. Before moving on, I must ask this question: Why do you think most financial advisors seem to emphasize portfolio management? It's because portfolio management is the primary source of their compensation. True wealth management is a process and much more than just managing a portfolio of stocks and bonds, mutual and exchange traded funds and any other tools thrown into the mix.

Portfolio management is just one component of what we do but it's not the only thing we do. We define portfolio management as a synergistic strategy for managing your investments based on your goals, risk tolerance and timeline. Choosing your investments is important but monitoring them over time within the context of life events is far more valuable in the long-term. Portfolio management is only one of the eight pillars, and it works in conjunction with the other seven to build your foundation for financial success.

Some years ago, well before we classified for ourselves what constituted a "good-fit client relationship," we had a prospective client referred to us. His sole objective was to only have his portfolio managed. Despite our pleadings that portfolio management alone does not constitute a fully viable wealth management plan, this prospective client stuck to his guns. An advisor can't possibly do a worthy or admirable job of financial planning for a client if most or all of the other seven pillars are overlooked.

All of the work involved in building a large, robust portfolio proved meaningless when the risk management pillar was ignored, leaving the client exposed to a lawsuit that annihilated a good portion of the assets. Despite our innate intentions to organize a client's financial affairs to protect and grow assets, this client insisted we stay solely in the lane of portfolio management.

Today, we no longer engage with any client – regardless of portfolio size – without a full commitment to addressing all aspects of their financial life. The lesson for this specific client was catastrophic, and for us, it clarified the importance of never letting a client's insistence override our better judgement.

Next, imagine the cost of ignoring the eroding forces of taxes while focusing exclusively on portfolio growth. We have seen the cumulative effects of tax erosion. It can constitute more than a 33% leakage in the growth of a portfolio by simply failing to address taxes in a mindful and proactive manner.

We understand that the portfolio is often the driving force behind wealth accumulation and wealth maintenance. However, without a total panoramic approach, investors can leave themselves open to all sorts of setbacks and deteriorations—most of which are unnecessary when anticipated and planned for accordingly.

Pillar 2: Income Planning

There are two distinct phases in every financial life cycle – the Accumulation Phase and the Distribution Phase. The two are very different in what they're designed to do, as well as how they are structured and managed for success.

The Accumulation Phase represents the years that you're saving and investing for your financial future. Management in this phase is largely dependent on your personal risk tolerance profile as it relates to managing and growing your portfolio.

The Distribution Phase is when your accumulated assets must be restructured to provide an income that supports you in retirement. Most financial advisors are capable of helping you in the Accumulation Phase of your financial life. However, very few have the knowledge, experience and expertise necessary to handle the critical Distribution Phase.

For many decades, the Distribution Phase was left to pension plans and Social Security - systems designed to generate an income for life. Today, few have access to built-in mechanisms for generating a lifetime income.

The distribution landscape has changed dramatically but distribution mechanisms haven't really caught up for clients whose goal is to build an income stream they can't outlive. In addition to longevity, a retirement distribution plan must address other challenges such as inflation, taxes and inevitable market volatility.

It is critical that the *financial sherpa* who got you up the accumulation mountain also possesses the necessary skillset for guiding you down the distribution side of the mountain, for this is where the real danger lies. Did you know that far more folks die on the descent down Everest than on the climb up the mountain? The same can be said of income planning.

Income and Distribution Planning is a highly specialized area of wealth management. Factors such as which accounts you rely on for income, what assets you utilize for income, and when and in what order your assets are converted to income can all play a huge role in how long your money will last in retirement.

You cannot take this area of planning lightly. It can mean the difference between a meaningful, fulfilled life during retirement vs. having more life at the end of the money. We will dive much deeper into this topic in

Chapter 5, as this area holds the key to much of your retirement cash flow success or failure.

Pillar 3: Liability Analysis

Credit is a fact of life. Most people have a mortgage, carry some credit card debt and many have utilized other forms of financing as well. Most people spend far more time, energy and effort managing their assets than they do their debt. The result is often an inconsistent, undisciplined and reactive use of it.

This pillar of our Wealth*Trac FORMula* is designed to help you manage your liabilities as a component of your personal balance sheet. Debt has become a bad word in many circles. However, when used judiciously, it can be a valuable tool in your financial life.

Healthy utilization of debt can help you to stabilize inconsistent cash flows. When something unexpected comes up, it can give you the freedom to take care of the situation without having to liquidate assets. In some situations, it can even be used to build wealth and help you achieve your financial goals.

In liability analysis, we assess your individual situation as well as your behavioral tendencies on both the asset and liability side of your personal balance sheet. We then take steps to safeguard against potential weaknesses, while leveraging the positive aspects of your financial profile to encourage better financial decisions.

Have you ever considered utilizing a line of credit when your portfolio may have suffered a drawdown? How about the opposite - have you leaned on a line of credit to avoid recognition of an untimely taxable gain? Credit and debt can be powerful tools in the right measure at the right time and for the right reasons.

Pillar 4: Tax Awareness Planning

Taxes can significantly impact your overall net returns - so much so that it can be the single largest wealth eroding factor we each face. Tax awareness planning is an important foundational pillar in our Wealth*Trac* *FORMula*. We are constantly examining and monitoring each component of your financial plan to determine potential tax ramifications and we work to develop strategies for reducing your tax liability.

Whenever and wherever necessary, we consult with outside tax professionals to ensure we are doing everything possible to reduce your tax liability and maximize your overall accumulation. No one likes to pay any more in taxes than they need to, and we want to protect your investment returns from a tax bite that is avoidable. Collaboration with your other professionals is key in this area.

Is your financial advisor collaborating with your CPA/Tax Advisor? If not, why not? This is a crucial area that cannot be overlooked without serious potential consequences.

Pillar 5: Risk Management

Risk management is a big term that can mean different things to different people. In portfolio management, it's about balancing the risk you can comfortably handle with the returns you require to reach your desired goals within your designated time frame.

However, in true wealth management, risk management is about much more than balancing portfolio risks with returns. It's centered around your life and the stakes are quite high. Risk management typically involves insurance planning with the goal of protecting you, your loved ones, your income and your property from the unknown.

A key and central component in risk management is ensuring that your loved ones are provided for in the event of your death. It's important that we take the appropriate measures to protect their lifestyle and the future you envision for them should something happen to you.

Another area of risk management we'll want to address with you is protecting your income should you become disabled or face unanticipated health issues during your working years. Again, this is primarily protection of lifestyle for you and your family.

In the case of long-term care insurance, risk management encompasses protection of your dignity and your assets. According to the Administration for Community Living (ACL), a part of the US Department of Health and Human Services, people turning 65 years old today have a 70% chance of needing some type of long-term care services at some point in their lifetime. On average, women need care for longer periods of time - 3.7 years vs 2.2 years for men and 1 in 5 will need care for longer than 5 years. [6]

---

[6] "How Much Care Will You Need," ACL, US Government, accessed January 22, 2022, https://acl.gov/ltc/basic-needs/how-much-care-will-you-need#:~:text=Someone%20turning%20age%2065%20today,for%20longer%20than%205%20years.

If you've ever had to deal with a family member transitioning into long-term care, you know just how expensive these services can be. As part of our risk management process, we work to make sure that you are protected.

If you're fortunate enough to have built a large enough asset base, long-term care coverage is less vital financially. However, often it is a relief to family members who must make decisions concerning mom or dad's care. Having a commercial insurance carrier on the hook to cover some, most or all of the costs associated with those long-term care needs can be a comfort to everyone involved. Consider the emotions involved when forced to choose between best of care for mom/dad or a reduction in your inheritance. Aren't the decisions a lot easier when costs are outsourced to a commercial insurance carrier when appropriate?

In February of 2022 my Mom passed, and her 9½ year long-term care benefit had run out almost a year earlier. This meant that her two sons (my brother and I) had to pick up the slack for that duration. While she was a woman of modest means, the coverage which she had secured in the 1980's afforded her the dignity of being able to remain in place as she aged from her mid 80's through her mid 90's. She never had to wonder if or where she might have to resettle. This was a comfort to her and I can assure you that it was a comfort to her two sons.

I gained two key takeaways from this experience. Long-term care needs can persist a lot longer than you might imagine and having coverage is not only a financial tool but an important psychological tool of support as well. You must not overlook or look past the three life contingencies: not living well enough, not living long enough and living a long, long time. In all three instances capital is needed to address the responsibilities of each of these contingencies in a noble and dignified manner.

Pillar 6: Estate and Legacy Planning

To many financial professionals, estate planning and legacy planning are synonymous terms since they both involve the transfer of assets upon death. Both are important but we make a very clear distinction between the two.

Estate planning involves things like having a will, a revocable family trust, a power of attorney and your healthcare directive for starters. It includes planning your end-of-life wishes and deciding how your assets will be distributed after your death. It's essential that you have clarity on these issues and have taken steps to have the proper legal documentation in place.

Legacy planning is far more holistic in nature. It is more about how you want to be remembered and what you want to leave behind that will continue on after you're gone. While transferring valuables is important, we've found that transferring value systems is equally important to our clients.

As part of our Estate and Legacy Planning, we'll spend the time to understand what's most important to you. It may be creating a trust to pay for your grandchildren's education, instituting special directives for family heirlooms, creating a strategy for seamlessly passing the family business you built along to your heirs or creating a charitable foundation to keep your philanthropic desires intact. It may even entail a special needs trust where the law allows for this type of planning and when a special needs child must be provided for.

Special needs children are growing in numbers that are startling. It is estimated that 1 in less than 60 children are born on the Autism Spectrum alone.[7] Whatever is important to you, we want to ensure that everything is in place to carry out your wishes in the way you envision for those you care about and will someday leave behind.

To leave a good legacy behind is really more about the value systems you leave than the valuables themselves. When you provide your heirs with proper instruction and guidance, they make their way through the world more smoothly than a rich, uninformed heir ever could. We help you have these discussions with your children and foster the values of good stewardship -- financial and otherwise -- in important family relationships.

Are your end-of-life final wishes written somewhere for your family to find so they know whether cremation or burial is preferred? Have you laid out many of the aspects that otherwise is left to your loved ones to figure out and agree upon? Have you thought about where to leave the legend to all your account passwords?

We provide a formatted *Personal Legacy Journal* for those not so inclined to record all the details themselves. Mark Colgin, CFP created this tool only after he lost his young wife at age 29. Even as a financial planner, he felt

---

[7]"Data and Statistics on Autism Spectrum Disorder," Center for Disease Control, accessed March 7, 2022, https://www.cdc.gov/ncbddd/autism/data.html.

the weight of not knowing exactly what his wife wanted or where to find all the things necessary to carry on with their young children. He didn't want his clients and others to experience such dismay along with such grief.

No more apt words could be said about estate and legacy planning than the insight shared by auto-sales trainer, Jackie Cooper when he conveyed *that it's the things you do that you don't have to do that always determine the difference when it's too late to do anything about it.*

Pillar 7: Philanthropy

As clients approach their goal of financial independence, priorities often begin to shift from "having enough" to "determining the type of legacy you want to leave." Charitable giving may become increasingly more important to you.

Although you can always donate to your favorite charities just by writing a check, you may become more interested in creating a legacy of giving to the charities that are meaningful to you. We explore other options for giving that may offer you tax benefits, while helping to create a lasting legacy of philanthropic giving.

Checkbook philanthropy is one thing and with it comes a tax deduction. However, did you know that the philanthropic portion of the tax code is there to incentivize greater charitable inclination and giving? Our US Government long ago saw the power and wisdom of promoting works of charity to the private sector. They realized how much more efficient and judicious spending would be in the hands of directly concerned and motivated citizens. This part of the tax code is often underutilized. Many times, tax and financial mechanics when combined can make 1 + 1 equal so much more than 2 for the donor and charity alike.

Does the advisor you've hired look through the lens of the philanthropic tax code to understand the many avenues and deductions you could be entitled to as you plan your financial affairs? This alone can add wealth to your balance sheet by eliminating an unnecessary tax loss with integrated planning techniques.

Pillar 8: Value-Added Services

In our Wealth*Trac FORMula*™, we are always looking for ways we can go the extra mile for our clients. Our goal is to always bring our clients additional value beyond your typical financial planning services.

What that looks like is as unique as our clients. Over the years, we have helped our clients with everything from planning family strategy meetings to reviewing executive compensation plans to helping clients gain clarity on business exit strategies and succession planning. We work tirelessly every day to earn the title of "trusted family advisor" - receptive to whatever path the trajectory of your life takes us on together. When we do this right, we are not only a trusted advisor, but soon become the "first call advisor."

This title is reserved for the few good enough to help regardless of topic and with a qualified network of resource partners to assist in navigating issues in and outside of conventional financial planning. The grieving widow, the new divorcee, the recent college graduate, the young budding family all get a hand extended as a result of our commitment to a co-navigated future with our clients. Who said financial planning should remain riveted solely to matters of money when a client's needs often extend far beyond the arena of finance?

Look through this lens of value-added services. Make sure you're confident that your advisor not only gives a clear hoot but has traveled these paths before. We feel deeply about community-building amongst our clients and do so intentionally and with great purpose. I speak more about this in a later section.

Wealth*Trac FORMula*

Our Wealth*Trac FORMula* is designed to continually adjust and monitor critical life and financial events to keep your plan on track. It's not something you can outgrow. It's a process that grows and evolves with you.

The process itself, the Wealth*Trac FORMula* focuses on the *Three D's:*

Discover
- What is essential to you?
- What do you want to accomplish?

Design
- How will we get you there?
- What services are the best fit for you?

Deploy
- Financial planning

- Customized strategy implementation
- Ongoing continuous service
- Building a lasting relationship on our shared journey

This is what we believe integrity should look like in wealth management. Everything we do is built around you and developing a deep and long-term relationship with you on this shared journey. We decided a long time ago to make the client's voice the voice we listen to, and the one that helps us stay true to course. True North is inescapable when what matters most to the advisory team is what clients value most.

We only want to be all things to a select group of clients who share our values of giving life our best and always seeing things through to completion. This is the standard for integrity that we have set for ourselves, and this is the standard you should expect in wealth management.

Looking through this lens, assess what you have and whether it fits as comfortably as it should. If not, you are now better equipped to spot truly integrated planning done with integrity.

Chapter 4

The Power of Collaboration

"Two is better than one when two can work as one."
— Coach K, Duke University
College Basketball Coach, Hall of Famer

G enerally speaking, most clients who come to see us have a close group of trusted advisors — typically a CPA, an estate planning attorney, a property & casualty insurance professional, along with some connection to a mortgage broker and sometimes, a private banking relationship. Each is concerned with assembling a specific section of the client's financial puzzle.

Unfortunately, what often happens is the client accumulates a lot of puzzle pieces without any picture of how everything is supposed to really fit together because the advisors rarely discuss the comprehensive picture. Have you ever tried putting together a puzzle without the photo from the box? It's nearly impossible to do. What makes matters worse is these professionals usually assemble their section of the puzzle independently and at different times or stages. This results in a high probability that it doesn't necessarily fit together at all. The client is then left with a plan - if you could even call it that- which simply isn't cohesive and integrated.

We believe in a more collaborative approach to life planning. In other words - it takes a village. This phrase is applicable to many different situations in life but it's especially true in wealth management. A truly enlightened and panoramic financial process necessitates an element of collaboration and often, an in-depth degree of collaboration.

The term collaboration is a broad one and can be defined in many ways – often differing in matter of degree. A financial advisor may answer phone calls or emails from a client's other advisors and although this is beneficial, it is not collaboration. It is merely communication. Wealth Advisors often work with other professionals to facilitate changes that they have made for a client - such as retitling assets in a trust or working with a CPA on required minimum distributions. However, this is not collaboration. It is coordination.

Although communication and coordination are both essential to the collaborative process, true collaboration exists on much higher level. According to the Oxford dictionary, the definition of collaboration is "the act of working with another person or group to create something." Our ultimate goal for collaboration as it relates to a client's wealth management plan is to integrate the collective wisdom and shared knowledge of their trusted professionals to create a life plan that also maximizes their *Return on Life.*

You need a catalyst - a quarterback - that takes responsibility for organizing the team on the field of play. Some clients do this naturally, but they are the rare exception. I have found absent a financial advisor serving as the agent of change, the client often continues dealing with these areas independently, never achieving the integration and integrity of the plan(ning). Having a *time*

& *responsibility chart* of *who* is going to do *what* by *when* allows for the path to have full integration – seeing things through to completion.

We leverage the insight we acquire in this process to help us achieve the client's wealth and lifestyle goals more effectively. Strategic partners we find ourselves most often working with include:

- Accountants
- Trust and Estate Attorneys
- Business Law Attorneys
- Business Valuation Professionals
- Retirement Plan Administrators
- Property and Casualty Brokers
- Mortgage Brokers
- Private Client Bankers
- Elder Law Attorneys/Special Needs Attorneys
- Commercial and Residential Realtors
- Commercial Bankers
- Tenant Representatives
- Other Subject Matter Experts (depending on the topic involved)

Trusted advisors are often considered experts in their field. However, expertise in any field can sometimes result in professional blind spots. Most experts become experts by adhering to a certain methodology and strategy in their specific area. Discussing ideas in a collaborative environment helps all of the advisors involved to avoid tunnel vision and develop a more unified strategy for the client.

And guess what? The more sophisticated the planning gets as wealth grows, the more important it is for a client's team of advisors to have a unified voice and cohesive message. Often, a client is expected to move into complex planning areas that they may not fully understand. This can sometimes leave them paralyzed and unable to move forward without a harmonious voice of allied advisors guiding them along.

As we have discussed in previous chapters, wealth management is much more than just choosing the right investments for a client's portfolio. To maximize your Return on Life, all components of your financial life must be considered and aligned with your unique wealth objectives into an integrated holistic plan.

When professionals fail to collaborate, it can be both confusing and frustrating for the client. Often they're left unsure as to what questions to ask of whom. For example, a client may think that all of their tax questions should be directed to their CPA. However, some tax matters may have legal consequences and should be discussed with an attorney as well. A wealth advisor may need to be aware of tax payments as they can impact a client's cash flow and net worth.

Insurance matters have all sorts of legal implications. Every investment decision ultimately results in a tax consequence. Dealing with these questions in isolation is insufficient and could even be considered borderline malpractice.

Further complicating the situation there are many areas that a client has little to no experience in and the decisions being made can be long-term and life-changing in nature. Rather than send our clients out to these other professionals on their own to decipher the next steps, we prefer to recruit and engage those professionals into our overall planning process. We never just give our clients a short list of professionals to "try on" - cutting them loose to determine which ones they can and should work with. Unfortunately, this has become a fairly common practice in the financial industry: speak with these folks and select one to work with.

At IWM, we literally shepherd clients through the process of formulating or modifying their wills and trusts. We have candid discussions with them regarding the dynamics and ramifications of their dispositive provisions – essentially the decisions of *who gets what, when they get it* and *in what form.* It is usually in the heirs' best interest to protect their assets from creditors and predators inside of an appropriate trust vehicle. We help clients with difficult decisions such as whether to roll out all or some of the money to beneficiaries (during life) giving the beneficiaries full control or explore other alternatives of storing assets in trust more permanently.

Many times, the client feels much more comfortable when we assist them in navigating the estate planning process with an estate attorney or the tax strategy planning with a CPA. While we don't profess to be the subject matter expert in these discussions, we do believe in serving as a client advocate - sometimes asking the questions that the client doesn't know to ask or is hesitant to ask for whatever reason.

We also serve as a sort of translator for the client on how a proposed solution relates to or impacts other plans already in place. Most importantly, we are there to ensure that the implementation of a specialized solution integrates well with their existing situation without compromising other components of their overall strategy.

In many instances we have discussed the long-term ramifications of selecting the proper tax situs for trusts so it may survive several generations. Some states allow trusts to live for hundreds of years or more. Many clients do not know that the trust vehicle itself can be a beneficial shield for asset protection against failed marriages and possible bankruptcies of current and future heirs to come.

We had one family learn firsthand the merits of shielding assets with proper trust planning. By having the appropriate trust in place, we were able to protect their grown child from a vindictive second spouse trying to harpoon a family business in a divorce filing after only 19 months of marriage. A properly drawn trust for correct and legitimate reasons can serve a family for many years to come, regardless of who tries to divert family assets. These tools are only helpful when the client is aware of them and feels comfortable enough to implement them.

Collaborating Through Life Stages

Every individual navigates through different life stages over the course of their life. The same is true of your financial life and the collaborative process functions differently at different stages of life.

One of our most important roles is that of "issue-spotter" on behalf of the client. Through years of experience and as stated earlier, we know that there are two primary things that can hurt us in life — *"what we don't know and what we know that ain't so."*

Imagine not being aware that an excess liability/umbrella insurance policy doesn't integrate correctly with the underlying homeowner's and auto liability coverage. This could leave a gaping hole where not only is a $5,000 deductible due and payable, but an additional $200,000 void exists between the auto policy's upper limit and the excess liability policy's inception limit which is often prevalent when carriers holding the coverages are not the same. That is a surprise that isn't always visible to the client and sometimes not even to the agents or brokers who may have assembled these coverages piecemeal — perhaps, primarily looking for bargain rates.

An airplane pilot will always tell you that *it's not the planes he or she can see that worry them – it's the planes that they can't see that worry them.* The financial advisor's job is to identify issues that a client may not even be aware of but have the potential to throw their plan off-course. As issue-spotters, we future-cast potential areas of concern that should be discussed *before* they ever happen. We're not clairvoyant, but there are practical and repetitive issues that we see over and over again that can in fact, be addressed beforehand to avoid their occurrence.

The Younger Family

A main priority for the younger family is to organize their capital and legal instruments. It's imperative that they formulate and formalize their estate planning documents. Their estate planning documents will basically fall on four pillars – wills, trusts, powers of attorney and health care directives.

Believe it or not - the average age of an individual when a first-time will and trust is drawn up is typically around 45 years old. If a young family comes through our door in their 30s and 40s and they don't have a will, they're going to get one through a licensed attorney of their selection. We take this seriously. We take them under our wing and in many cases, even drag them through the process to completion. It's never a maybe or maybe-not question. It's a must-do and we are with them every step of the way – guiding them and advocating for them in discussions with their legal professionals.

Did you know that it is estimated that more than 50% of Americans don't have even a basic will according to www.caring.com? And the younger the group, the less likely they are to have a will. This is inexcusable for people who have some means - especially, when there are minor children involved.

As stated earlier, there are two essential components upon which our firm philosophy is built - sincerity to family and sincerity to finances. It is part of our narrative in every conversation we have. Not dictating an asset minimum as a standard allows us to employ our philosophies with integrity to this group who may not as of yet achieved well-heeled balance sheets. We respect and admire the two values that we hold dear, especially in a young couple striving to get ahead. We will do everything we can to help them protect their family and ensure their family's financial success.

Just the other day, I was in a conversation with a young woman who asked about the firm minimums. I explained to her, "We don't define our minimum in a form or fashion that you're probably used to hearing such as asset levels or household net worth. We base our minimums on a client's commitment to the sincerity of their family and a sincerity to financial success."

We have witnessed time and time again that those two sincerity components are more often than not, the underlying "why" for people who are successful. They might not be successful today in the traditional sense but if they remain focused on those two elements, they are what we call "emerging wealth." They will inevitably grow their wealth while doing the right things for their family and that's important to any advisory firm.

I tell my kids and anyone willing to listen several things about achieving financial success: "It's like a magnifying glass. You must get it in focus and hold it steady to generate any real heat and energy." And to that I add, "Always remember, it takes most of us about 15-20 years to become an overnight success. Don't ever forget - discipline is what lasts long after the excitement of the moment if you're going to gain any follow-through."

Once the appropriate legal documents are in place, we turn to financial components and for a young family, the initial financial components are there to address life's contingencies and answer three questions. What happens if I don't live long enough? What happens if I don't live well enough? What happens if I live a long, long time?

We address all three of these contingencies within the context of every family's economics. We examine their balance sheet and financial statements and ask the difficult but critical questions. Do you have enough money for your family to survive the calamity of a premature death of the breadwinner(s)? More than likely that answer will be no at this early stage, which necessitates an instrument to backstop that contingency – life insurance.

If your income were to stop because of an infirmity or disability, could your family survive and maintain their present lifestyle? If the money or capital is not on their balance sheet today, we make provisions to protect them through disability income replacement coverage.

Finally, if the individual is healthy and going to live a long, long time, they will need capital for that natural and likely circumstance, which means saving and investing.

We then make resource allocation decisions around money to augment savings and investing.

For the young family, we are essentially helping them to organize their world. We get them started with systematic investing. We believe that you should invest out of capital and systematically save out of income. Most young couples don't have a lot of capital to make investments, so we get them set up to make their auto-contributions and it doesn't really matter what they start with, just that they start. Once they begin, they'll see incremental success which in time, becomes exponential success. This is when we discuss giving themselves a raise by helping them figure out how they can then make larger periodic contributions – whether pre- or post- tax is also analyzed.

Many of our younger families are children of our older more established, wealthier clients. Many of these younger families strive to be independent of their parents' wealth, never losing sight of the value of their own hard work, enterprise and industry. While they know full well that mom & dad will likely leave them significant assets, their solid upbringing and current disposition propels them forward on their own success trajectory. This is so encouraging to witness as these children are continuing the productive, enterprising legacy that their parents established decades earlier.

Collaborating Through Mid-Life

In the middle of life, many people begin to think in terms of transitioning to retirement. If they've been with us since the beginning, everything should be in order and we monitor their situation. However, if they came to us in this middle phase of life, like the younger couple, we help them get their capital and legal instruments in place.

In this middle stage of life, the burning question is centered around retirement. Will I have enough money to live on when I retire? We calculate the math behind that question and discuss what that actually means in real terms.

Once we've determined that they have the assets required to support their retirement, their next question usually revolves around the "how" of the question. How do they optimize distributions? Do they postpone taking money from their IRA until a later date or do they take it early before their required minimum distributions kick in? Do they utilize funds from their tax-deferred bucket? Should they pull money from life insurance on a tax-free basis? Was any of their savings in the form of a Roth and should that be tapped into or postponed indefinitely?

We work through the financial gymnastics of calculating and developing an optimal income strategy. We do not offer tax advice but we are diligent by remaining tax aware in our income strategies and decisions. When clients have significant asset complexity, we recruit the CPA to advise on all sorts of issues that could involve things like restricted stock units or old incentive stock options, deferred comp supplementary retirement plan (SERP) aspects, etc.

In this stage of life where assets have grown substantially, we often bring in different subject matter experts around the different areas. Entrepreneurs who want tax deductions may want to explore captive insurance trusts. Charitably inclined individuals may need to consider the various tools available: charitable annuities, charitable lead and remainder trusts, pooled income funds, and donor advised funds to name a few.

When retirement becomes imminent, it is a pivotal time in clients' lives. They can sometimes reach a point when they've outgrown their advisors. This is a time when they need to observe their financial landscape from a different point of view to see potential pitfalls, as well as opportunities. In these cases, we do not hesitate to call in subject matter experts wherever and whenever we deem it necessary.

As the old saying goes: "If you think education is expensive, try ignorance." Having qualified expertise saves not just heartache, but in my experience, it can save significant amounts of money and time.

Collaborating Through The Retirement Years

In this life stage, discussions become much more focused on the long ball – after the client is gone. Of course, the subject of retirement was discussed when they were in their 50s and 60s but once they reach their 70s and 80s, the discussion takes on a new importance and urgency.

Most clients in their 80s accept that a transition is inevitable and may not be far off. Hopefully, they still have another good decade, maybe even two, but thoughts typically turn to legacy planning at this time.

As little as twenty-five years ago, we lived in a time of the male-dominated autocratic leader. He wasn't around as much due to building a business/career, but he still made all of the financial decisions for the family. Typically, if he was out building a business or working endless hours at the office, he was unavailable to instill creative thinking, forecasting and future-casting into his family culture. Often, this leaves a void where one parent is forced to cultivate vision and culture alone.

In contrast, creative leaders today work throughout their lives to instill a money value system into their family. Children are invited into discussions to talk about the impact of money in their lives with both parents. When clients are purposeful and intentional about sharing their money values with family, they tend to hand off much stronger value systems to the next generation. We've touched on it in previous chapters, but we have found over the years, it's not so much about the transition of valuables but rather, the transition of a value system that truly leaves a legacy.

We wear many hats with clients during this stage. As they work through legacy issues, we often act as facilitators and mediators with family and continue in our role as advocate and consultant with their trust and estate planning attorneys.

It's not unusual to have elder care issues also arise during this time. If we start to sense that a client may be diminishing in capacity, we act quickly to have consent forms signed for the client's designated persons of interest. This protects everyone involved so we can engage in sincere discussions with and about mom or dad, whose capacity may in fact be diminishing. This is a time when they should have a support system around them. It benefits everyone to have another set of eyes and ears watching and listening when decisions of significant magnitude are made.

We have a client with Parkinson's Disease. Before he was on medication, he was showing signs of diminishing mental capacity. However, once his medication was adjusted, he started to come back brilliantly. Now, at times, he's beginning to fade again. By having his persons of interest in place, as the advisor, I can speak with the two sons and three daughters openly. In this case, as in many, the kids are not local. I may detect issues that they may not be aware of and speak to them of my concerns. The client's wife is older than he is and doesn't necessarily have a grasp on financial issues. This couple is from the male-dominated era, and she chooses not to be any more involved than necessary. For almost 60 years, financial issues have never been part of her world. Involving capable and caring adult children can ease the burden for this spouse in having to solely make difficult decisions.

Each stage has its own emphasis and idiosyncrasies. Being prepared to travel along and traverse the varied stages of the client's life is what separates "first call" advisors from a mere portfolio manager. Look more closely through the lens of Financial True North to determine what should be inherently built into the landscape of comprehensive wealth management for you and your family. Be certain that you are aligned with the proper firm to help you navigate through each of the financial life stages that you will face. There can be great disparity among outcomes when your advisory team is not integrating their planning with your other professionals and family members.

Chapter 5

Accumulation, Distribution And Retirement Income

"Getting to the summit is optional, getting down is mandatory."

– Ed Viesturs

We touched on this topic in Chapter 3 when discussing two of the eight pillars of wealth management. However, this topic deserves its own dedicated chapter given its vital importance.

From your first day at your first job - even if it's with your own company - until the day of your retirement party or the sale of your business, the financial rules of the game are fairly straightforward and understood. You work hard, enjoy life, provide for your family, maybe buy a few toys along the way, but you never take your eye off of the ultimate prize – financial independence and the work-optional lifestyle it can provide.

The goal during your working years is to amass as much money and assets as is practical in your investment accounts and maybe even max out your retirement accounts, depending on your personal situation. If you appreciate the power of outsourcing and delegating to a subject matter expert, you hire a wealth manager you can trust to keep you on track, avoid pitfalls and help you to make wise financial decisions all along the way. Your mantra is "total return" and size *does* matter when it comes to retirement savings and financial freedom.

You've worked hard and decide it's time to take advantage of the work-optional lifestyle that makes work discretionary or even obsolete. You've grown a nest egg that you can be proud of – only now, all of the rules change and they change dramatically. You move from earning an income to support your lifestyle, to now relying on assets in your portfolio of stocks, bonds, real estate and whatever else you may have accumulated to produce the income necessary to drive your anticipated lifestyle. In fact, it's not just the rules that have changed – it's more like the whole gameboard has changed. All of the financial lessons you learned in the "accumulation phase" of your financial life cycle are turned upside down when you enter this new, unchartered "distribution phase."

Successfully producing retirement income takes planning and is a lot like the descent from Mt. Everest as mentioned in Chapter 3. There have been many books written on how to get up the mountain, financially or literally – how to prepare mentally and physically, potential obstacles you'll likely face and situations to look out for. Other books describe the journey to the top - the discipline required and the sense of accomplishment and relief you feel when you're finally standing on top of the world.

The way down is a different story. Very few books are written on how to get down the mountain safely and with all of your appendages still intact. Interestingly enough, most of the accidents, injuries and deaths on Everest occur on the way down as noted earlier. After the euphoria of summitting the peak of Mt. Everest, many people tend to be less diligent and let their guard down. This can lead to disaster. Often, people don't recognize just how much the rules differ on the descent.

The same is true in retirement planning and income distribution. You're no longer relying on earned income and now must shift to generating passive income. The truth is, many advisors can probably get you up the retirement mountain because those rules are not only well known, but they are fairly straightforward. Most of their training and experience relates to the accumulation phase of planning. Although some advisors are more skilled and comprehensive in their preparation, most can likely get you at least close to the summit - assuming they have properly calculated the actual elevation you need to scale financially.

However, the knowledge and expertise required to get you down the mountain safely and without running out of money is far more challenging. It takes specialized training to integrate tax, financial and market variability or volatility quotients. This necessitates a unique skillset geared toward distribution optimization that most advisors just don't have.

In this chapter, we'll take a closer look at the accumulation and distribution phases of retirement planning. We'll examine how they're different and what is required in each phase to be successful.

Accumulation Phase

The Accumulation Phase of your planning can be defined as the income-producing years that you spend working and contributing consistently to your investment and retirement accounts and perhaps, acquiring property. It's in this phase that you're generating a steady stream of earned income which provides you with a multitude of options in terms of investment vehicles and strategies. If you happen to experience a setback during this phase, you can compensate for it with time because you're still earning a regular income.

Achieving a relatively steady rate of return is a critical factor in your ability to accumulate lasting wealth. Not losing money is just as important as making money and sometimes, even more essential in the long-term.

Consider this example: you have a dollar, the dollar grows by 50%, how much do you have? Next year that sum shrinks by 50%, how much do you have then? If you said a dollar you might want to think it through again. You see, the dollar first grew to $1.50 in that first year and then it shrunk by 50% leaving with only 75 cents. Not losing money is far more impactful to your long-term results than making money because of the perils hidden in the math.

Compound growth during the Accumulation Phase has a way of taking care of itself as long as your asset base can avoid wild downward swings. We're all familiar with the old adage of starting early to invest for your future. Having time on your side, along with a prudent investment strategy can provide long-term positive returns without ever having to "push the envelope." In fact, nothing can effectuate death blows to a portfolio faster than pushing the envelope by taking on excessive risk in the hopes of creating aggressive growth or "beating" the market. When an asset shrinks dramatically and sometimes even to zero it takes a monstrous rate of return just to break even again. Lose 25% and you need 33 1/3% to get even. Lose 50% and you need a 100% return to just get back to even.

When you have the discipline to start early and can remain diligent over the course of your earning years, you're usually rewarded with significant long-term returns. The longer you spend in your Accumulation Phase, the more you're insulated from bear markets – you have time to utilize the opportunities they offer in maximizing bull markets.

The decisions you make in the accumulation phase of your financial life cycle will directly affect your ROI (Return on Investment) and your ROL (Return on Life). Decisions such as when you start, how much you invest, how often you invest and the investment choices you make have a direct impact on how and when you'll retire. More importantly, they will dictate the quality of life you'll experience in retirement.

The Accumulation Phase of retirement planning is often characterized as a race to grow your retirement savings as much as possible during your working years. Often, success is measured by account values alone. We believe there's a lot more to it than that.

Like most things in life, having a healthy balance is key. We work to help you balance your Return on Life with your long-term retirement goals. Our Wealth*Trac* *FORMula* helps us to gain crystal clear clarity on what's most important to you now and in the future. This gives us the ability to plan accordingly throughout your accumulation years and make the best decisions possible through all phases of your financial life - regardless of what curve balls life may throw your way.

Look through the lens of integrated planning where portfolio gains alone do not measure success: are you getting answers and clarity on the totality of how the accumulation of assets alone is not success? At least it's not the success or path you'll need as you begin your descent down the other side of the mountain in the Distribution Phase.

Distribution Phase

Retirement is typically one of the lengthiest chapters of your life. People retiring at age 65 can easily spend 30+ years in retirement. You can expect to experience many changes as you transition into your golden years. However, your most challenging adjustment will likely be the shift from a regular and predictable income to living off of your savings...for the rest of your life. This requires not only a mental shift but an emotional one as well.

The Distribution Phase actually begins long before you ever take your first withdrawal. The process starts with a complete analysis of your nest egg in its entirety - what investments you hold and in what type of accounts you hold them. Your investments will generally require much closer supervision in this stage of your life. In the Distribution Phase, you must be concerned not only with your investments, but also with the timing and amount of distributions to ensure the longevity of your retirement savings.

All of your financial life, you've lived by the rules of accumulation and growth. It's important to understand exactly how those rules change as you enter the Distribution Phase and your focus shifts to generating and providing for income. The same tried and true concepts of time and compounding which were on your side in the Accumulation Phase now have very different effects when the focus is on producing income.

Your primary objective is no longer growth alone. The goal now is to generate enough income to provide for your spending without running out of money.

Market volatility was your friend in the Accumulation Phase. It gave you the opportunity to buy more shares when markets were down and grow your wealth when they turned back up. However, this is not the case in the Distribution Phase.

When the market is down and you're withdrawing fixed dollar amounts, more shares must be sold to provide the same amount of income. This can erode a portfolio value more rapidly than you may think. It is sometimes referred to as *reverse dollar cost averaging.* These disadvantages are far worse on the downside than the constructive power it served on the upside during the accumulation period.

Markets are always fluctuating – up one day and down the next. Did you know that markets on a daily basis are up 54% and down 46% of the time measured by the S&P 500 Index according to *Equitable* research?[8]

When you're in the Accumulation Phase, corrections in the market may be stressful but not as consequential as they are in the Distribution Phase. As we mentioned previously, time is on your side when you're focused on growing your assets. You have the luxury of time to help you recover before retirement savings are called upon to support you.

However, in the Distribution Phase, market corrections can significantly impact the ability of your retirement assets to provide enough income over the long-term. If market corrections occur early in retirement

---

[8] Michael A Higley, "By the Numbers," *Equitable*, March 21, 2022.

when you're just starting to depend on your assets for cash flow, a market dip can have a devastating and lasting effect on retirement income. This is called the *Sequence of Returns Risk.*

Age	"Up" Market—Mr. Green Annual Return	Year End Value	"Down" Market—Mr. Brown Annual Return	Year End Value
65		$1,000,000		$1,000,000
66	5%	$1,050,000	-25%	$750,000
67	28%	$1,344,000	-14%	$645,000
68	22%	$1,639,680	-10%	$580,500
69	-5%	$1,557,696	16%	$673,380
70	20%	$1,869,235	21%	$814,790
71	19%	$2,224,390	5%	$855,529
72	23%	$2,736,000	-16%	$718,645
73	9%	$2,982,240	8%	$776,136
74	16%	$3,459,398	14%	$884,795
75	23%	$4,255,059	24%	$1,097,146
76	22%	$5,191,172	14%	$1,250,747
77	-26%	$3,841,468	5%	$1,313,284
78	-15%	$3,265,247	-15%	$1,116,291
79	5%	$3,428,510	-26%	$826,056
80	14%	$3,908,501	22%	$1,007,788
81	24%	$4,846,541	23%	$1,239,579
82	14%	$5,525,057	16%	$1,437,912
83	8%	$5,967,062	9%	$1,567,324
84	-16%	$5,012,332	23%	$1,927,808
85	5%	$5,262,949	19%	$2,294,092
86	21%	$6,368,168	20%	$2,752,910
87	16%	$7,387,075	-5%	$2,615,264
88	-10%	$6,648,367	22%	$3,190,623
89	-14%	$5,717,596	28%	$4,083,997
90	-25%	**$4,288,197**	5%	**$4,288,197**
Average Return	6%		6%	

Figure 5.1
©2016 Robert W. Baird & Co. Incorporated. Member NYSE & SIPC.
Robert W. Baird & Co.

In the first table (Figure 1), the average rate of return is held constant on both sides using the same identical returns only reversing the order of those annual returns for Mr. Brown and Mr. Green. You can see that when accumulating and climbing the mountain, the order or sequence of returns doesn't matter. It only matters that the returns generate an average of 6% compounding over the 25 years in both columns for Green and Brown.

Now look at Table 2 (Figure 2). The earnings rates are the same as in Table 1 for both Mr. Green and Mr. Brown but now you can see the impact that the sequence of returns has when depending on a portfolio to generate income. In the first instance, Mr. Green's portfolio more than doubles over the 25 year period of time while Mr. Brown skids precipitously off the slope. Mr. Brown runs out of money well before the calculated age of 90. In fact, by age 83 there is less than the full $50,000 available to withdraw in that year. This is still several years short of the average life expectancy for a male and much shorter than for a female of similar age.

Age	"Up" Market—Mr. Green			"Down" Market—Mr. Brown		
	5% Annual Withdrawals	Annual Return	Year End Value	5% Annual Withdrawals	Annual Return	Year End Value
65			$1,000,000			$1,000,000
66	$50,000	5%	$1,000,000	$50,000	-25%	$700,000
67	$50,000	28%	$1,230,000	$50,000	-14%	$552,000
68	$50,000	22%	$1,450,600	$50,000	-10%	$446,800
69	$50,000	-5%	$1,328,070	$50,000	16%	$468,288
70	$50,000	20%	$1,543,684	$50,000	21%	$516,628
71	$50,000	19%	$1,786,984	$50,000	5%	$492,460
72	$50,000	23%	$2,147,990	$50,000	-16%	$363,666
73	$50,000	9%	$2,291,309	$50,000	8%	$342,760
74	$50,000	16%	$2,607,919	$50,000	14%	$340,746
75	$50,000	23%	$3,157,740	$50,000	24%	$372,525
76	$50,000	22%	$3,802,443	$50,000	14%	$374,679
77	$50,000	-26%	$2,763,808	$50,000	5%	$343,412
78	$50,000	-15%	$2,299,237	$50,000	-15%	$241,901
79	$50,000	5%	$2,364,199	$50,000	-26%	$129,006
80	$50,000	14%	$2,645,186	$50,000	22%	$107,388
81	$50,000	24%	$3,230,031	$50,000	23%	$82,087
82	$50,000	14%	$3,632,235	$50,000	16%	$45,221
83	$50,000	8%	$3,872,814	$50,000	9%	$0
84	$50,000	-16%	$3,203,164	$50,000	23%	$0
85	$50,000	5%	$3,313,322	$50,000	19%	$0
86	$50,000	21%	$3,959,120	$50,000	20%	$0
87	$50,000	16%	$4,542,579	$50,000	-5%	$0
88	$50,000	-10%	$4,038,321	$50,000	22%	$0
89	$50,000	-14%	$3,422,956	$50,000	28%	$0
90	$50,000	-25%	$2,517,217	$50,000	5%	$0
Average Return		6%			6%	

Figure 5.2
©2016 Robert W. Baird & Co. Incorporated. Member NYSE & SIPC.
Robert W. Baird & Co.

For many, it may not always be obvious how much more treacherous the descent down the distribution side of the mountain is. However, let's be honest about two things: a) rarely does one withdraw a flat amount from their portfolio over a two-and-a-half decade period of time. Some escalation for inflation must be built in. Fortunately, Mr. Green has some margin for error with a growing portfolio value. Mr. Brown on the other hand, would have seen his portfolio crater well before age 83, assuming a meager 3% Cost of Living Adjustment to his withdrawal amount each year to accommodate purchasing power maintenance.

In real life one does not see a cliff ahead and keep driving straight toward it without regard. In finance, if you perceive the cliff ahead and a portfolio heading toward self-destruction, I suspect you would drastically reduce the level of income you are distributing or withdrawing from the portfolio.

Rarely, does anyone continue withdrawing at the same level while observing a precipitous drop in portfolio value year after year. However, a decrease in the distribution amount taken from a portfolio, regardless of whether taken annually, quarterly or monthly isn't a reality most wish to confront in their golden years.

This may not be an actual failure, but it's a failure nonetheless when the golden years turn bronze. As I stated in my introduction - failure (of any sort and any magnitude) is just not an option when it comes to your finances.

It is critical that your plan and planning consider sequence of return risk throughout retirement. Your advisor must build in the necessary structures and design elements around market volatility to protect you from either falling off the financial cliff altogether or having to dramatically ratchet down your distribution levels in retirement.

How does the plan address inflation? Is there any reliable rising income component? Not too long before we went to publication, measured inflation in the United States was running 2-3 times above historical norms.[9] At an inflation rate of 6%, money's buying power shrinks approximately in half every 12 years vs at a 3% inflation rate, money takes roughly 24 years to slowly shrink to half its buying power.

As of the beginning of 2023, the United Sates national debt stood above $31 trillion with no stoppage in sight.[10] Is there anyone who doesn't feel tax rates will rise? Net after-tax spendable income takes on a whole new meaning as we navigate a super debt-laden economy and the taxing implications associated with such.

After a complete analysis of what you have in retirement savings and where you have it, the next area

---

[9] "Monthly 12 Month Inflation Rate In the U.S. From January 2020 -January 2023," Statista, Accessed February 19, 2023, https://www.statista.com/statistics/273418/unadjusted-monthly-inflation-rate-in-the-us/#:~:text=In%20January%202023%2C%20prices%20had,data%20represents%20U.S.%20city%20averages.

[10] "Our Debt Clock" Truth in Accounting, Accessed February 19, 2023, https://www.truthinaccounting.org/about/our_national_debt?gclid=EAIaIQobChMI_P2an4Gl_QIVGxbUAR1gIA-pEAAYASAAEgKb8_D_BwE

we examine is how much you'll need in regular income to live the retirement lifestyle you've always dreamed of. After all, success in retirement should be measured by quality of life.

Estimating Retirement Expenses

One of the most debilitating mistakes retirees can make lies in underestimating their expenses in retirement. Your current expenses are always the starting point. First, we look at which expenses will remain the same and identify which ones are likely to change as you enter retirement. It's important to also factor in the expenses you may not incur now but will have to take on once you're no longer employed - medical/health insurance, auto, travel, etc.

Next, we evaluate the spending that will likely decrease in retirement. For example, your transportation expenses may go down since you no longer have to make that long commute every day. However, your firm's auto allowance may be gone. Clothing expenses are another area that may decrease as you no longer have to dress for success. You may also eliminate or reduce that weekly dry cleaning bill.

Many retirees think once they retire and are on Medicare, their healthcare expenses will decrease significantly. This is rarely the case. In fact, healthcare expenses typically rise as you grow older. Often, Medicare supplements come very close and can even exceed the out-of-pocket costs you were paying in your employer's healthcare plan. Long-term care insurance is something many retirees should have and most will utilize at some point in their retirement.

Another important area we address when evaluating client expenses in retirement is how much you want and can afford to assist aging parents and help children/grandchildren financially. While this is every bit financial in scope, it is also at least partly philosophical in terms of whether parents feel a need to reach down and assist children financially. Most of our clients feel a sense of responsibility, while a few feel it is robbing the children of their own motivation and the full experience of hard work, even the struggle to succeed. If you choose to help, this should be clear in your own mind, budgeted for prior to retirement and discussed with children so everyone is on the same page. If these guidelines are not firmly established ahead of time, it can lead to family turmoil, in addition to being a serious drain on your retirement income.

Finally, we look at lifestyle spending. What do you want to do in retirement? What's still on that bucket list that you'd like to check off before leaving this earth? Those bucket list items may change considerably as you progress through the different stages of retirement.

Immediately after you retire, it's normal to have a lot of pent-up desires. Suddenly, you have the time to do all the things you've always wanted to do or buy the things you've waited a lifetime to enjoy. You may want to travel or buy that new sports car or take up that new hobby, all of which is fine. However, it's prudent to prioritize these desires and budget for them because this is only the first phase of retirement.

In the next phase of retirement, most retirees begin to stick closer to home and family becomes the priority. For many, this is the lowest cost phase of retirement, but it can vary considerably depending on the size of your family and your degree of involvement.

The last phase of retirement is dictated by your health. For most, healthcare costs rise dramatically in this final phase of retirement. According to the National Institutes of Health (NIH), per capita lifetime expenditure is $316,600, a third higher for females ($361,200) than for males ($268,700) with 50% occurring during the senior years. [11] This means that total medical costs amount to more than $134,000 from age 65 alone if you are a male with a shorter life expectancy. And combined, the total for a husband and wife from age 65 forward is estimated to be more than $314,500 - and that's in today's dollars.[12] There must be accommodation for rising costs along the way as you progress through retirement and medical expenses creep up more rapidly than core inflation rates.

Putting Together A Plan

When we have clarity on your retirement assets and your estimated expenses in retirement, we can begin to structure a retirement income plan for you. There are a multitude of different retirement income strategies that are available today – some more sophisticated than

---

[11] Berhanu Alemayehu and Kenneth E Warner, "The Lifetime Distribution of Healthcare Costs," Health Services Research, Accessed March 19, 2022, ohttps://www.ncbi.nlm.nih.gov/pmc/articles/PMC1361028/#:~:text=Per% 20capita%20lifetime%20expenditure%20is,half%20during%20the%20senio r%20years.
[12] Ibid

others, and the viability of many are dependent on the size of your retirement asset pool.

Regardless of the income plan designed, it's essential that we always remain acutely aware of the potential impact of this monthly income on your taxes. Which accounts you take from can have a dramatic effect not only on your taxes and Medicare premiums. Not being judicious in where you draw from can also have an impact on the longevity of your retirement assets.

Next to healthcare, taxes are typically one of the largest expenses retirees will incur. Each of your retirement and investment accounts may be taxed differently depending on the timing of withdrawals. Therefore, it's so important to be strategic in how and when you take income from each account. Left to chance or poor planning, you risk a whole lot of possible and unnecessary tax leakage.

Taxes and how they relate to retirement income planning is beyond the scope of this book. We are not tax advisors, nor do we profess to be tax experts. That's a job for your CPA or tax attorney. However, we remain tax aware when structuring retirement income plans. We collaborate with your tax professionals to make sure any potential tax bite is addressed and together, we will work collectively on your behalf to calibrate that optimal solution.

The Bucket Approach to Retirement Income

The bucket approach, sometimes referred to as the "time segmentation strategy" is one of the simplest and more popular retirement income strategies. It involves setting up different "buckets" or accounts for different pools of assets. The investments chosen for each bucket are dependent upon the time frame in which they'll be used.

Money required for immediate and near-term income would be held in cash and cash equivalents. Your mid-term bucket would contain more balanced, total return types of investments such as bonds, CDs or dividend-generating conservative funds. Because your immediate income needs are being met, your longer-term assets in the third bucket can be invested for growth so that they continue to build and your overall return stays ahead of inflation.

This strategy usually gives investors the confidence to allocate a portion of their retirement assets to true growth but sacrifices in low interest rate environments a great deal of total return. However, when you know that your immediate income needs are taken care of, you usually feel more comfortable letting the longer-term money bucket be invested in riskier, higher return potential investments. However, it's important to remember that only a portion of the money invested is achieving those potential returns - no guarantees can be made.

Systematic Fixed Percentage Withdrawals

This is the strategy most advisors default to when structuring retirement income plans because it's relatively easy and it's what they know. With the increased volatility and what had been lower interest rates in the financial markets over the last ten years, this strategy has fallen out of favor.

In this income plan, you leave your retirement assets fully invested in some asset allocation mix and liquidate a fixed withdrawal amount, typically 4% each year to meet your income needs. The logic behind this strategy is when your assets grow by more than 4%, it will offset the years in which your portfolio earns less than 4% and it all evens out in the end.

For most of the last decade, interest rates have remained at historical lows which has fueled much debate over whether that 4% figure is too much or too little. The problem with this retirement income strategy is it has a built-in uncertainty factor when most retirees are looking for more certainty in their retirement income strategy.

Combining Tools of Investments, Life Insurance and Annuities to Develop a Broader Mix

One of the options that your advisory team should also explore is how you might utilize various tools and approaches in different measure to hone in on a more appropriate overall solution set. It is rare that one solution or toolset can withstand or address all situations and through all personal and economic scenarios that one may encounter. Having the flexibility to access and incorporate the various tools available within the financial universe may more adequately achieve an optimal strategy and be in the Best Interest of the client.

Keep in mind that if life insurance and its inherent attributes are to be considered it usually needs to have been put in place years earlier in anticipation. Future casting is critical to this approach. *Integrity's* agnostic and unbiased approach allows intelligent well-tested thinking to prevail, rather than any predispositions to a specific strategy. Thus, one must always resort to running the numbers. The economic consequences should be evaluated under various scenarios to weather-test the variability of outcomes. This ensures that the client has the most complete information possible on which to base his or her decisions.

Testing, Measuring and Verifying

The primary objective of a retirement income plan is to structure it so that it will last longer than you do. The second most important objective is that you receive income at a rate that allows you to have and maintain your ideal retirement lifestyle.

The Bucket Approach to Retirement Income and the Systematic Fixed Percentage Withdrawals strategy are two of the most popular and commonly used paths for providing retirement income that we see. However, there are other approaches that we have found valuable.

Every strategy you are considering should be *tested, measured and verified* in a financial calculator, financial planning software or financial simulator. Keep in mind that no one of these alternative approaches to retirement income generation must be your one and only path. There's no reason why these various strategies and even others cannot be combined if the combination increases the benefit to you while possibly also safeguarding against risks and exposures.

Regardless of which path or combination of paths you choose, the most important thing is to be sure that a financial professional has run the numbers to test, measure and verify potential outcomes. In this process, several factors should always be examined. The predictability of cash flow; the tax consequences generated as a result of that cash flow and the duration and sustainability of the cash flow. All of these must be considered carefully.

Your advisor should be able to calculate and articulate to you the consequences of a specific retirement income strategy in language and in numbers you can understand. When making a decision on which approach or combination of approaches to use for retirement income, take the time necessary to understand exactly what you're doing and why you're doing such at least on a basic level. It's one of the most important decisions you will make.

Remember - the game completely changes when you move from accumulation to distribution in your financial life cycle. The advisor who can help you up the retirement mountain may or may not be the right person or the proper firm to help you navigate down that same retirement mountain safely without running out of money. This is just one example of why it's so important that you have a wealth advisor who has experience in retirement income planning.

An experienced retirement income planner can usually structure your retirement income in a way that not only may help increase your income distributions but may save you money on taxes as well - all of which may be validated by your tax advisor.

There's little room for error once you enter retirement and are into the Distribution Phase. The right knowledge, experience and expertise in this area has the potential to completely change the course of your retirement. The stakes are high in the retirement income game. This decision has the potential to significantly impact your income and quality of life in retirement. Don't take this area lightly.

Chapter 6

Service, Service, Service

"To give real service, you must add something that cannot be bought or measured with money and that is sincerity and integrity."

– Douglas Adams

"Make the voice of the client the voice you listen to."

Duncan MacPherson

O ur Wealth*Trac FORMula* is specifically designed to be a process that you'll never outgrow as you progress through the different stages of your financial life. Rather, as I've stated several times already, it's a process that you grow into – one that grows with you as regular and critical events in your life unfold.

We are 100% committed to this shared journey that we are on together. Continual, ongoing service and maintenance are key components to ensuring that your plan remains fluid and dynamic enough to evolve as you do. It becomes less about *The Plan* and more about *The Planning* along the way.

This is not a "set it and let it" program, nor is it one that goes into effect only when you have a concern. The families we work with do not utilize our expertise in isolated instances. They understand and appreciate that we are helping them chart their own course to financial success as well as preserving that same success.

Your life is unique and your life events will unfold in their own unique ways. Our primary purpose is to ensure that nothing takes you by surprise. We respond to all of your life and financial circumstances with compassion, and our Wealth*Trac FORMula* process gives us the tools to respond with individualized solutions that fit you, regardless of the situations you may face.

Our entire staff work as issue-spotters for your plan. We like to think that we monitor your plan against life events with the same diligence and precision as an airline pilot. We are continually scanning for potential turbulence and initiating a system of course corrections whenever we encounter negative feedback or information that indicates we could be moving off-course.

Failure is not an option. I cannot emphasize this enough even at the risk of being redundant. Just as pilots say to their passengers: *If you don't arrive safe, we don't arrive safe.* We remain in contact with you regularly through our regimented service calendar. Go to: **https://www.integrityiwm.com/our-services** to get a copy of our service menu.

Remember, we all live by the rules we set. We decided long ago that we will always make ourselves available *whenever* a client has a specific concern. You are never alone on this journey when your goals and objectives are aligned with integrity.

Everyone faces critical life events – both positive and negative at different points in life. No one is exempt. These are acute issues when they arise – someone dies, a child or grandchild is born, a new marriage or a looming divorce, the sale of a business, an inheritance, or an illness or disability. Events like these can change you and at times, can rock you to your core.

How you adjust and adapt to these events when they occur can have long-term ramifications. We are always with you – evaluating your options, celebrating your victories in good times and guiding you to find minimally disruptive solutions in the not so good times.

Market events can potentially have the same emotional effect. The market drops 35% in a single month as in the pandemic of 2020. What do you do? We are always with our clients - talking them through it – helping them to determine the course of action that is right for you. For some, it may be "let's wade in a little deeper because this is a buying opportunity." For others, the conversation may be more one of "let's hold the course." And in extreme instances, it's "let's tact the sails and take a different course."

Very few of our clients would choose to de-risk out of the market in that scenario because they know that we are here to help navigate stormy weather with them and for them. This "never alone" mentality that we instill in all of our clients usually gives them the confidence and peace of mind to weather the market storm and allow it to pass.

Remember that the odds of an up day in the market measured by the S&P 500 index was 54% in your favor and 46% against you. Do you know the odds grow substantially in your favor the longer the time frame? Measured in months it's 61% in your favor, 39% against. During a full year, it's 74% in your favor.[13] That's close to the markets showing positive gains three out of every four years. If a casino offered those kinds of odds, how much and how often would you wager your good money?

The only truth that squares with history is this: declines are temporary and advances are permanent. There is no escaping that truth no matter how bearish or pessimistic one may become. At the time of this publishing, there have been 27 market corrections since World War II. And within every trading year there is a pull back from peak to trough of approximately 14% on average measured over the past forty years.[14]

---

[13]Michael A Higley, "By the Numbers," *Equitable*, March 21, 2022.

[14] Marquit, Miranda, "What Is A Market Correction," Forbes, Update September 23, 2022, https://www.forbes.com/advisor/investing/what-is-a-market-correction/#:~:text=There%20have%20been%2027%20corrections,in%20the%20index%20of%2013.7%25.

.

We also regularly track progress against your financial mile-markers. It's important to us that we know at all times where you are relative to the goals you've set. Are we ahead? On-course? Behind or off-course? Evaluating this information on an ongoing basis gives us the ability to proactively course-correct sooner rather than later.

The monitoring and maintenance elements are critical. Make sure your advisor has a system to follow or you can risk getting further off course than necessary.

Raising Financially Astute Children

Family is important to us – your family and our client family. It is the cornerstone of our mission, philosophy and value system. In fact, as you may recall, the "F" in Wealth*Trac FORMula* stands for Family.

Because family is as important to our clients as it is to us, it's not surprising that we often hear questions about how and when to begin educating children on money. The question we hear most often is, "How do we get our kids to start thinking in this area?"

Our answer usually begins with that age-old right of passage for children called allowance. We encourage our clients to start instilling their value-system around money from an early age. A solid first step is to position allowance not as an entitlement, but rather something that your children must earn by completing chores around the house.

Then we share our *"Three S"* philosophy of money with them. The *Three S's* are *Saving, Spending and Sharing.* We suggest that as part of the allowance process, they give their children three mason jars or envelopes and earmark one for each "S."

We want to instill in children early on that their allowance, and any money they receive for that matter, is not designed for consumption alone. All money that they receive should be divided into each of their three containers—whether equally or disproportionately is up to the parents.

It's also up to the parents to provide guidance on appropriate allocations and educate them on why each container is important. The child's spending container is for money that they can enjoy now. The saving container is to invest and enjoy in the future and should entail a discussion on the merits of delayed gratification. This leads to lessons on what a bank account and an investment portfolio is and ultimately, provides hands-on experience with these instruments funded by their accumulation of savings. The sharing container helps them to understand that there is a community that they are a part of, and it extends beyond their own consumption. They can make a difference and be involved in giving a hand-up to others less fortunate.

We encourage the parents to have ongoing conversations with their children around the saving and giving container. Ask them what they're choosing to save for, why and how long they think it will take to save for their desired item. You may also want to illustrate different saving rates and show them how allocating more of their money to the savings container could help them get to their saving goals faster.

When discussing their sharing container, it's a good idea to suggest that they do some basic research on how they'd like to donate their sharing money. This also gives the child a sense of purpose.

Make this a project of importance so that your children learn early about the significance of being connected to something bigger than just themselves and getting involved in causes that are important to them. Be creative; have the child do the research on various charitable organizations and have them present a short report to you on what the organization is, who it serves and why they choose to support this sort of mission. You may want to ratchet up their motivation by electing to match dollar for dollar the child's donation to the selected organization(s). The sky may be the only limit when it comes to being a good citizen of the earth.

This approach puts children on a healthy and stable financial path early in life. You've educated them on thinking more globally and past solely their own consumption. They begin to see that there is a whole world out there and they can have an impact on it. Besides a wonderful educational experience, it's a fun, sharing experience for both parent and child.

When you instill the value of philanthropy into a child early, it's something they will carry with them for the rest of their lives. What parent doesn't want to raise a child who is socially conscious and cares about people and the world they live in?

Sounding Board Process

I started this career with a mind for helping people. Few things give me more satisfaction professionally and personally.

Our clients know that we are their biggest advocates and are always looking out for them. Our highly personalized approach and consistent contact gives our clients the confidence to view their future with anticipation and confidence rather than apprehension and anxiety.

This isn't necessarily the case in every advisor-client relationship. Separating noise from signal can be tricky especially when facing a major life transition. What was once clear can become cloudy and confusing especially when an event is emotionally-charged. Without professional experience, guidance and compassion, it's easy to lose sight of your True North and make critical mistakes that can haunt you for many years.

In these circumstances, we offer our Sounding Board Process as an additional service to our clients. When they have friends, family or colleagues who are feeling apprehensive about their future or perhaps, experiencing a critical financial or life event, we will meet with the people they care about to review the situation.

Common life events that are often triggers and require clear navigation may be:

- Death of a spouse

- Marriage or divorce
- Sale of a business
- Retirement
- Illness or disability
- Inheritance

These events are sometimes predictable. However, when they are unexpected, this adds an element of stress and emotion which is rarely beneficial when important decisions must be made.

Because we want this process to be as seamless and comfortable as possible for everyone involved, we offer these guidelines to our clients when they wish to offer this service to someone they care about at no charge or obligation:

- Begin by sharing the benefits you feel you've received from being part of our *WealthTrac FORMula* process
- Ask their permission to initiate the conversation with us
- Give us a call to share general information about the friend or family member they'd like us to contact
- We will reach out to them on your behalf

- We will send them an introductory kit so they don't feel intimidated and know more of what to expect
- We will follow up and schedule a Sounding Board Meeting

We never approach these meetings as a client-building exercise for our firm. In fact, those who are introduced cannot become a client in that meeting. If at some point in the future, these folks wish to engage in further discussion about their situation and we feel that it's a good fit on both sides, we'll set up a follow-up meeting. However, the sole purpose of the Sounding Board Process is to be of service to our clients and to those they care about as advocates for a better world.

Your Return on Life, and the happiness you strive for, as well as those you care about, is the work we're committed to. Everything we do is rooted in what matters most to our clients. We really "see" you and work to understand you better in every situation and with every year that passes. This is the kind of relationship we have with our clients. This is what integrity looks like to us. We couldn't imagine it any other way.

Peer through the lens of service as defined here. Are you finding this level of resolute commitment in your provider(s), financial and otherwise? If not, you deserve better. It's out there for those no longer willing to settle for something less than authentic and integral service.

Chapter 7

Client Community

"Never doubt that a small group of thoughtful, committed citizens can change the world: indeed, it's the only thing that ever has."

— Margaret Mead

A s we mentioned in the very beginning of this book, our ideal clients are not defined by investable assets alone, but rather by attitude and values. They are a lot like us. We genuinely like them and enjoy the time we spend together. Our ideal clients value relationships and demand trust - they are engaged and willing to take steps to improve their situation and the situation of those around them.

We no longer take on non-ideal clients for reasons that have less to do with our own pomposity and more to do with keeping the hull of the ship always righted for the greater good of those already onboard—our current clients. You see, non-ideal relationships can lead to drains and drags on the entire system making it that much tougher to deliver best-in-class service to our existing clients who deserve our best.

We had to learn this the hard way, but today it is a rule of engagement. We screen properly before committing to a working relationship since the future and the journey are shared for many years to come. In this way we preserve the integrity of our delivery system to all of our clients.

Throughout the year, we host a number of educational and social events to bring this amazing community of people together. During Covid, we had to curtail many in-person events, but learned how to hold our clients' attention in a virtual environment. We learned much from the challenges of the pandemic when it comes to managing client relationships and successfully running the operation virtually. We hope we never have to face another such challenge, but we are ready should the situation arise.

What we've found is, our clients genuinely like and enjoy each other's company. These are bright and successful people – many are business owners and professionals who ultimately end up doing business with each other.

Our events are the perfect venue for our client community to get and stay acquainted and close. Often, friendships develop. It's not unusual for us to see hugs and big smiles when they greet each other at events which we've been running for almost two decades now, (except for the interruption of Covid). Many get together outside of our venue on their own and we've even seen some go on to do their own events together for causes that they believe in. It's as inspiring as it is warming to know we had a hand in changing outcomes and impacting lives for the positive.

I must share the story of a very successful Wendy's franchise owner we'll refer to as Charlie. This entrepreneur owned more than 50 Wendy's stores in the mid-South. One day in a meeting some years ago, he said to me, "It must be amazing to have a job like yours meeting successful business owners and professionals and learning all about them - what makes them tick, how they got successful and what they're doing to continue that success professionally and personally."

Wow! Here's a guy who has accomplished amazing financial and personal success and he's telling me - a 30-something-year-old young advisor at the time how fortunate I am to be in my profession. What he was actually saying about just how lucky I was to be in such a position didn't hit me immediately. It took some maturing and a few years before I understood the gravity and accuracy of what Charlie had said to me on that fortuitous day.

The experiences continue to be so wonderful and impactful with insights and lessons beyond my wildest dreams. I am grateful to Charlie for being humble enough that day to point out how special it is to be a financial advisor, connected to such a tremendously successful and industrious group of people on a regular basis.

Client Events

We love to entertain and we like to think that we're pretty good at it. Typically, we host a few major social events each year – one during the summer and one around the holidays. Our most recent summer get-together had a Caribbean theme and many dressed accordingly. We hold a client appreciation high-end wine pairing sit-down dinner in the early summer and a Holiday Open House in December.

Food and drink are always plentiful and everyone has a wonderful time deepening relationships and enjoying each other's company. At that Caribbean themed event recently, the steel drum band played while a phenomenal strolling magician made his way around the room, dazzling everyone he interacted with.

Our events are a wonderful opportunity for clients to relax and socialize. We like the idea of building a community of successful people who have the ability to make a difference in the world.

We have an interesting group of clients - artists, musicians amongst the more conventional professionals. One of our clients even owns a gondola company. From the gondola company owner/operator to our resident cantor client from the local temple who was classically trained, we have more than our share of well-tuned voices to serenade when the paid entertainment takes a break. We are fortunate to have such wonderful talent woven into the fabric of our client community.

Prospective clients are from time to time invited to these events. They are always amazed at the caliber of people who are part of our client family and often, after they've had an opportunity to mingle with this diverse group of people, they want to become a part of what we do.

In addition to our social events, we offer many educational events throughout the year. We ask and we listen to what our clients are interested in learning more about. Our market-related events are timely and on topics that our clients have clearly expressed an interest in.

Not all of our educational events are centered around purely financial topics. From time to time, we'll bring in guest speakers who have expertise on health matters or world events that may have an indirect effect on planning or financial issues.

Because taxes and estate-planning issues are always moving targets and a topic that affects everyone we work with, we bring in experts to speak on new regulations when appropriate. These workshops and discussions are designed to give clients additional information and suggestions in these specialized areas.

Women's Council

As mentioned previously, we noticed some time ago that a lot of wives were not accompanying their spouses to the meetings with us. The husband made all the decisions and drove the agenda, the wife rarely joining him in our meetings. Because women generally live longer than men, we felt that this dynamic was not in anyone's best interest. We knew it was quite probable that these women would be making the financial decisions at some point in their life.

Even with some of our same sex couple clients, the contrast of dominant leader vs follower becomes apparent. We think it's important that there is co-authorship in their own household's financial future. We do all we can to encourage the less dominant spouse/partner to be part of defining the journey.

It's important to us that we are relevant to both partners, as well as to the couple unit itself. We feel an obligation to educate the partner who may have been the traditional stay-at-home spouse raising the children in their family. We want to help build their confidence in the financial planning process. From experience, we know that a family who understands these issues together harmonizes better both financially and otherwise.

To course correct, we decided that we would host a women's weekend brunch. We invited several women from our client family and simply told them that we wanted to get their input on how we could be more relevant to them and their specific needs: *What did they want to see? What did they want to hear? What were their concerns and how could we best address those concerns in an environment that felt safe and comfortable to them?*

The feedback we received was invaluable. We chose some leaders from the group of attendees and asked them to help us form and author the future of this group, since we saw a vision of convening this group with some regularity going forward. They were excited to help, and our Women's Council was born.

Our plan is to hold meetings two or three times a year for this group. Recently, we had a panel of female trust and estate attorneys share valuable information with the group and answer questions.

A funny thing started to happen. These inquisitive women went home and began questioning their husbands on the information they were learning - *do we have this?*

We thought it would be an excellent idea for husbands to be part of the women's educational process. Husbands were encouraged to accompany their wives and now, you'll see both spouses at these meetings.

We're very proud of our Women's Council. Our original vision was that the group would become a safe place where women could be empowered as they grew in their financial knowledge and confidence.

Don't get me wrong, many of our female clients are independent powerhouses. However, for the back-seat spouses who never voiced or aired their opinion so specifically or clearly, this has helped crack the shell. Now, both voices are co-authoring and taking responsibility for the household finances.

Some husbands even expressed their relief that their spouses were now more fully engaged and helping bear the load of making sometimes tricky and difficult financial decisions for the family. These responsibilities formerly fell to the husbands simply because there was no model in their household to do anything differently. We had no idea when we began that it would evolve into a venue that would strengthen the financial bond between spouses and the family as a whole.

Advisory Board

Our Client Advisory Board (CAB) is currently more male-dominated because it has its roots in a decade and a half of history. Oddly, it is not comprised of clients exclusively although we refer to it as such. Some on the board are simply friends of the firm – historically, CPAs, attorneys and other allied professionals.

The Board began about 17 years ago. We thought it would be a great way for us to deepen our relationships with a select group of clients and receive valuable feedback from people who are important to us. There are but three things we ask of our CAB members.

First, we simply ask members to come to the meetings with their thinking caps on. Remember, these are seasoned individuals who are bright and experienced. They already show up poised for healthy, in-depth discussions because of their own life journeys. In the meetings, we share some of our thinking on ways we can add value and make more of a difference in the lives of our clients and our community.

The voice of our clients is always the voice we want to listen to. They provide their feedback on the ideas we share. It serves us well to test our thinking before running too far down the road with things that may not be received well by our client base.

Next, we ask Advisory Board members to be a beacon in the marketplace for us. When they see or experience anything that catches their attention, we ask that they share it with us. We're always interested to learn more about what they discover from other sources that they feel we might be able to leverage in our business to increase value.

We learn a lot about our competition and how to improve our own deliverables. We have a saying: "When you're green you're growing; when you're ripe you're rotting." It's best to think green in more ways than just one.

Third, we also ask our members to become ambassadors of goodwill for the firm. From time to time, someone asks for references when considering joining the community of IWM clients. Rather than choose a random person from our full clientele, we ask that Board members be open to taking the call and having a conversation with people who have an interest in joining our client family. Sometimes prospective clients have questions they would like to ask of a solid reference. Our Board members serve this role well because they know the firm more intimately than most clients due to their service on the advisory board so they can speak with authority.

We want to be part of our clients' lives because they are a big part of ours. We don't do what we do to simply acquire clients. We do it to build relationships that grow stronger with each passing year. We do it to build family – yours and ours. We are about, as our email signature line has indicated for years: Changing Outcomes and Impacting Lives (all for the positive).

Don't short change your experience with anything less than an integrated process that embraces you and your success with a deep commitment. Look through the lens of community to see your Financial True North through to completion.

Chapter 8

Roadmap Checklist To Financial True North

"A prudent question is one-half of wisdom."
— Francis Bacon

I wrote this book for people who value integrity in their relationships. It's absolutely critical to your success that integrity exists in any relationship with any wealth advisory firm that you choose to do business with – including the one you're with now.

This book explains what it means to have comprehensive advice. I've outlined how to select a firm with a robust enough approach to embrace and deliver true wealth management, rather than simply the financial idea du jour.

As life itself seems to accelerate in pace with each passing day, time continues to become a scarce and precious commodity. Because I feel so strongly about the subject matter outlined in this book, I've condensed the key concepts covered into a cliff note version that gives you a tool that you can begin to use immediately.

The stakes are high. Your family relies on you to seek best-in-class solutions and with the *Roadmap Checklist To Financial True North* presented in this chapter, you'll know how to spot it quickly and easily.

This checklist is your roadmap to determining if your current advisory firm or the one you are considering is truly meeting the standards of comprehensive advice. You no longer have to trust instincts – yours or a friend's. You no longer have to base your decisions solely on whether an advisor appears to be a nice person or seems trustworthy.

The checklist tool provides a methodology for quickly referencing the material and meaningful points in the book. Your finances and the financial advice you follow on your road to your financial goals is no place to settle. It's important that you are savvy in distinguishing between fully integrated and comprehensive intentions versus the advisor's revenue-centric ambitions.

Comprehensive advice in finance is rarely linear. Integration and the interconnectedness between seemingly separate areas is not as clear as many clients may think. For instance, every investment decision has a tax implication. Every estate planning decision has a legacy component – some with tax implications and some requiring actual title changes.

It is said that no man is an island. The same is true when it comes to finance. Very few financial elements stand alone and isolated from impacting other important areas. An advisor who lacks knowledge and experience or chooses not to address these matters in a comprehensive manner leaves the client with inferior outcomes in an increasingly complex world.

There's no shortage of financial advisors out there. Knowing how to pick the right one is not always a simple task. When evaluating financial advisors and wealth advisory firms, take the time to ask yourself the following questions.

Roadmap Checklist To Financial True North

1. Can the Advisor articulate the Scope of their work in a concise and understandable manner? *Seems simple, but take note of how convoluted and incomplete the responses are that you receive when you ask this specifically.*

2. Does the Advisor have a service menu that they can share with you outlining their services and the likely timing of those deliverables throughout the year? *This should be in writing and readily available before any engagement commences.*

3. Does the Advisor have the expertise and tools to calculate, illustrate and explain in a language you can understand what the implications are of a specific financial decision and its impact on your current and future cash flow, tax flow and net worth? *If modeling isn't done by this Advisor and the advisory firm, then who is going to do the modeling to test, measure and verify before you launch down any path?*

4. Although an Advisor may have been referred by a friend or family member, seems like a nice person and appears to be trustworthy, are they properly credentialed or earned the degrees necessary for acquiring advanced knowledge in a specific area of finance? *A true professional displays a commitment to their education, in addition to an ongoing pursuit of continuous education. This should be immediately obvious and apparent as most accomplished Advisors hold their degrees and credentials out prominently.*

5. If you are yourself a business owner is the Advisor also an entrepreneur or leader within their firm giving them a similar and unique understanding of the struggles and challenges you face in running a business and are they capable of providing real world solutions for both financial and nonfinancial issues? *Empathy for your personal and professional circumstances is crucial when someone too, has walked in shoes similar to yours.*

6. Does the Advisor embrace and aspire to the unstated role of Personal CFO to ensure that there is a clear integration across all aspects of your financial affairs? *Are you in this together or is this a transactional relationship solely for the Advisor? The difference is huge.*

7. Does the Advisor elevate to the level of viewing your working relationship as a *Shared Journey* and *Shared Future* with the sincere commitment required to ensure that you both get across the endline safely and smoothly - always willing to work tirelessly to make the necessary course corrections along the way? *No greater professional relationship can exist than when the client and Advisor are on a shared path into the future - sharing responsibility for outcomes.*

8. Does the Advisor have a curious and inquisitive mindset to explore and evaluate both inside and outside-the-box solutions that may be required to reach your financial goals? *The conventional answer is not always the correct and optimal solution. You should not have to settle for only*

standard stale and pale answers. It's important that you are made fully aware of all possible options before deciding on a path.

9. Does the Advisor take the comprehensive approach necessary to address a panoramic view of your financial needs: *tax management, estate planning* and *debt analysis* while simultaneously maintaining an eye for *risk management* at all times? *Comprehensive advice means just that—it should not start and end solely with portfolio management. There is so much more to successful, integrated wealth management – you should not stop until you find this for you and your family.*

10. Does the Advisor interact and collaborate throughout the year with your tax and legal professionals when appropriate to make your life and planning easier and better integrated? *This one benefit makes a world of difference in workload and efficiency for the busy person; never mind, the possibility for advanced and synergistic thinking.*

11. When it's beneficial to you, does the Advisor care enough to accompany you to important meetings with your allied professionals such as your CPA or attorney or are you left to attend those meetings without the benefit of your Financial Advisor present? *If you are walking into these discussions and meetings without your Advisor – both you and your advisor are likely achieving subpar results with those professionals.*

12. Does the Advisor possess the generally straightforward skills necessary to accumulate and build assets as well as a thorough understanding of the more challenging task of distribution planning in retirement? *This requires a very specific skillset and without it, the distribution phase has the potential for exposing you to a world of disappointment and grief during your precious retirement years.*

13. Does the Advisor understand "sequence of return risk" together with the concept of "reverse dollar-cost averaging" and the potential impact on your

retirement income strategy? *My suggestion here is to simply ask the Advisor to explain these two concepts and then determine if you are satisfied with their response. You'll know fairly quickly if the advisor displays a mastery of the subject or not.*

14. Does the Advisor have a willingness to assist children and family members in your household, regardless of whether they meet some financial threshold minimum? *More than likely, you are part of a family unit and your Advisor should see you as such and be willing to work with younger (and older) generations for continuity of care.*

15. Does the Advisor have a methodology for fostering and supporting the transfer of your *value systems* around money and finance to the next generation so that children understand more than just the *valuables* and assets that they will inherit someday? *Is there any methodology for preparing heirs for the wealth that may suddenly become theirs with the passing of a parent or grandparent? Preparation is key to*

avoiding all sorts of unfortunate outcomes that sudden wealth can create.

16. Does the Advisor have a deep desire to know and understand you better? Can they help you to articulate the "Why" as well as explain the "How" in language you can understand? *Intention is sometimes more important than method I have found.*

17. Does the Advisor encourage the development and execution of your lifelong bucket list so that you do get your desired ROL - Return on Life as well as your ROI - Return on Investment? *Do you have an expressed or unexpressed bucket list? If not, why not? Find an advisor who truly cares about turning your dreams into reality, rather than exclusively centering every discussion around portfolios.*

18. Do you understand clearly how your Advisor is compensated/paid? *Is it in writing for your review? If not, don't walk, run.*

19. Does the Advisor understand, and leverage opportunities present in the philanthropic area of The Tax Code to enhance potential outcomes for yourself and your favorite charities? *If you are unaware of how doing good (for others) can help you also do well, then you are missing a key ingredient in advanced tax mitigation awareness planning. You have the potential to create a lasting legacy when you learn to become "wisely" charitable.*

20. Does the Advisor have a grasp on *Special Needs Planning* elements and associated resources to help in this area, knowing that presently, 1 in 60 children are diagnosed with Spectrum related Autism each year? *If special needs concerns are not something that has impacted your family, then it may not seem important. However, more and more families face these challenges and comprehensive support extends beyond just professional and therapeutic help. It may also become a necessary component in your financial planning. Don't hesitate to seek out this specialty*

in your Financial Advisor if it's something that will benefit you and your family.

21. Does the Advisor and the Advisory Firm make the voice of the client the voice they listen to for input and feedback on firm direction and client care? *Are you a co-author of your Advisor's future trajectory or are you just along for the ride? How much input you are permitted to express and how much is heeded, is a good indicator of whether the firm is the right long-term fit for you. Your life evolves and your advisory firm should evolve with you. There is no reason why you should not or could not be a contributing author of that future.*

22. Is it obvious that the Advisor and the Advisory Firm sees things through to completion on most first attempts? *This is the core of what it means to have integrity in my opinion.*

23. Does the Advisor demonstrate the wisdom and experience required to be an issue spotter and identify gaps and potential hazards before they become real threats? *How far ahead is your*

advisor thinking when discussing your situation? Are they future-casting to see where obstacles could surface, and are they providing guidance on a plan to course-correct long before the road gets bumpy? Pay close attention to what they say and more importantly, what they don't say - you'll soon know if they possess this skill.

24. Does the Advisor understand the different tax implications and therefore, offer flexible compensation methods in terms of fee for service vs. commission in certain circumstances? *This can sometimes make a dramatic difference in your tax picture and you should understand the differences before you choose, or are defaulted to one method or the other.*

25. Is the Advisor aware of the differences between conversations around the family business vs the business of family when it comes to money and legacy? *This takes either advanced training or real-life experience to master. There is no faking it. Is the Advisor prepared to go deep with you and help you manage both objectives smoothly?*

Just like everything else in this book, the *Roadmap Checklist To Financial True North* is comprehensive in nature. If you would like clarification on anything included in the checklist or have any questions about the checklist, we'd be glad to answer them for you. Simply contact us by phone at **949-955-1188** or you can email us at: **inquiries@integrityiwm.com**.

Consider the *Roadmap Checklist to Financial True North* your GPS in determining if a financial advisor and their firm have the tools, knowledge, experience and approach required to be your navigator on a shared journey to your financial goals. Below you will find the QR for a free download of the *Roadmap Checklist To Financial True North.*

Integrity @ Work Checklist

Conclusion

*"The greatness of a man is not in how much wealth
he acquires but in his integrity and his ability to affect
those around him positively."*

– Bob Marley

I n this book we've discussed Return on Investment and
Return on Life - but your Return on Integrity is the
foundational principle upon which everything else is
built. It's hard to enjoy a return on anything, if integrity is
not present.

The principle of integrity is universal in nature and
scope. Whether consciously or subconsciously, it is the
value that we all seek in the people we interact with, and
the companies we do business with. It's what clients
search for in advisors and advisors search for in clients.

At Integrity Wealth Management, it's more than just
a core value. After all, Integrity is part of our name and it
is the basis upon which every decision is made and every
action we take. As I have reiterated throughout the book

- we hold integrity as a standard not just for ourselves but for our clients as well.

In the wealth management industry recognizing integrity isn't always as easy as it is in some other professions. Choosing a financial advisor is a critical decision for you and your family. It can be one that you celebrate for generations to come, or unfortunately, if based on chemistry or family connections alone, it can be one that shortchanges you on all that this kind of relationship could mean to you and your family. I've always believed that clients just don't have enough exposure to advisors to clearly understand the contrasts among professionals. As a result, too often they settle for a "good guy, doing what they believe is a decent job" when so much more is possible.

My hope is that this book will serve as a guide for you when navigating the sometimes opaque terrain of wealth management. Throughout the book, we've painted a very specific picture of what a comprehensive approach to wealth management should look like for you and your family.

The world and markets continue to change rapidly and exponentially. Old school advisors, firms and strategies following a firm-centric or revenue-centric model will not only fail you - they can be costly.

Our new reality necessitates a panoramic wealth management approach that is about much more than your investment portfolio. It must address all pieces of your financial puzzle - from tax and risk management to legacy and estate planning. Most importantly, you must have an advisor and firm that understands and possesses the income planning expertise to lead you down the retirement slope safely and without running out of money. On your financial success journey, collaboration with your other trusted advisors is not just preferred, it is essential.

Your financial picture is as unique as you are. *You and your best interests* should be at the center of every decision and every conversation that you have with your financial advisor.

This is precisely why we don't attempt to be all things to all people but rather, all things to a select group of people. Although setting asset minimums is the industry standard, we view the practice as self-serving and indicative of a revenue-centric focus.

Our clients are people who are passionate about family and finance. They also possess a level of asset sophistication that can derive the maximum benefit from our panoramic approach to wealth management.

Our Wealth*Trac FORMula* is our foundation and it all starts with the *FORM* in *FORMula - Family, Occupation, Recreation and Money* because that's what we've identified as most important to our clients. From experience, we know that the plan is not nearly as important as the ongoing planning which is why we developed a planning structure that's flexible enough to evolve with you throughout your life. It gives us a tool for facilitating our anticipatory role as "issue-spotter" and helps us to identify potential trouble before it happens.

Demand for integrity is increasing at a time in history when it's needed more than ever, yet supply can sometimes be difficult to find and discern. When you find it in an advisor relationship, hold onto it and nurture it – it's critical to your long-term financial success. Integrity is not an important thing. It is everything.

Business Coach, Dan Sullivan more preferably billed as the Strategic Coach said in class one day something I'll have never forgotten. "You'll be 95% ahead of the pack by doing four simple things in life that few others are willing to do: a) show up on time; b) say please & thank you; c) do what you say you are going to do; and d) finish what you start." I couldn't have captured the value and virtue of integrity any better nor more concisely than what Coach said that day about living productively on this earth.

Peering through the lens of Integrity makes all the difference in the world. Hold your financial and personal affairs to these standards and success will arrive and stay with you and your family for generations to come.

I have given you guideposts and a lens through which to assess and measure what you should be seeing in your relationship with your financial advisor. I trust that if you follow True North you will chart a course to even greater success.

ABOUT THE AUTHOR

Ralph Adamo began his career in the financial services industry in 1985 and quickly recognized that clients require broader services and a personalized plan to address their concerns and needs in today's complex world. His clients soon realized that he had an inherent ability to go beneath the surface and understand the deep emotional elements underlying financial issues. Those clients referred their friends, family and colleagues to him and his portfolio of business grew steadily.

Over the years, Ralph prepared himself to address the increasingly complex array of financial services required to deliver a truly comprehensive and far-reaching multi-generational wealth management program. He acquired the well-respected ChFC, CLU credentials, along with a Masters of Science in Financial Services (MSFS) from The American College. He is also an Investment Advisor Representative (IAR).

Driven by his singular focus on helping clients achieve their lifelong financial goals, Ralph has established successful long-term relationships with clients in many fields of endeavor nationwide. He strives to be a highly effective specialist on his own, but often serves as a catalyst for creating top level integration of a client's overall wealth plan by working collaboratively with the client's team of professionals. His goal is always to achieve results that exceed expectations.

Ralph is passionate about acquiring knowledge and applying it wisely. He founded Orange County's Chapter of Advisors in Philanthropy and was President 2012-2014. He also served as a Board Member of The International Association of Advisors in Philanthropy from 2011-2014. Ralph is the author of the eBook, *The Survival Guide for Serious Investors.*

In 2003, Ralph Adamo formed Integrity Wealth Management and began developing what became the proprietary *WealthTrac*™ process. He has built a team of professionals that provide clients with a collective experience and insightful creative strategy to help achieve their lifelong financial goals.

Ralph has been a resident of Orange County, CA for most of his adult life. Ralph is an enthusiastic supporter of local educational and charitable programs in Orange County, such as Habitat for Humanity, Families Forward and CHOC Children's Hospital. He is also proud Chief Emeritus of his daughter's Indian Princess Tribe and past coach to his son's soccer team.

Bibliography

ACL, US Government. "How Much Care Will You Need." Accessed January 22, 2022. https://acl.gov/ltc/basic-needs/how-much-care-will-you-need#:~:text=Someone%20turning%20age%206 5%20today,for%20longer%20than%205%20year s.

Alemayehu, Berhanu and Warner, Kenneth E Warner. "The Lifetime Distribution of Healthcare Costs." Health Services Research. Accessed March 19, 2022. ohttps://www.ncbi.nlm.nih.gov/pmc/articles/P MC1361028/#:~:text=Per%20capita%20lifetime %20expenditure%20is,half%20during%20the%20 senior%20years.

Anthony, Mitch. "Repositioning Your Value From ROI to Return on Life." Accessed January 14, 2022.

https://www.mitchanthony.com/repositioning-your-value-from-roi-to-return-on-life.

Center for Disease Control. "Data and Statistics on Autism Spectrum Disorder." Accessed March 7, 2022. https://www.cdc.gov/ncbddd/autism/data.html.

Higley, Michael, A. "By The Numbers." Equitable. March 21, 2022.

Inspirational Words of Wisdom. "Earl Nightingale Quotes." Accessed December 19, 2021. https://www.wow4u.com/earl-nightingale2/#:~:text=Integrity%20is%20the%20seed%20for,the%20principle%20that%20never%20fails.&text=If%20a%20person%20is%20working,that%20individual%20is%20a%20success.

Marquit, Miranda. "What Is A Market Correction." Forbes. Updated September 23, 2022. https://www.forbes.com/advisor/investing/what-is-market-correction/#:~:text=There%20have%20been%20

27%20corrections,in%20the%20index%20of%20 13.7%25.

Mercury News. "How Selling Too Soon and Never Buying At The Bottom Might Actually Make Sense." January 18,2018.https://www.mercurynews.com/2018/0 1/18/how-selling-too-soon-and-never-buying-at-the-bottom-might-actually-make-sense/.

Monevator. "Life Expectancy for Couples: Why It's Surprisingly Long and What You Should Do About It." May 29, 2019. https://monevator.com/life-expectancy-for-couples/.

Oxford Reference. "Dwight D Eisenhower Quotes." Accessed 12/17/21. https://www.oxfordreference.com/view/10.109 3/acref/9780191826719.001.0001/q-oro-ed4-00004005.

Statista. "Monthly 12 Month Inflation Rate in the U.S. From January 2020 – January 2023." Accessed February 19, 2023,

https://www.statista.com/statistics/273418/una
djusted-monthly-inflation-rate-in-the-
us/#:~:text=In%20January%202023%2C%20price
s%20had,data%20represents%20U.S.%20city%2
0averages.

Truth in Accounting. "Our Debt Clock." Accessed
February 19, 2023,
https://www.truthinaccounting.org/about/our_
national_debt?gclid=EAIaIQobChMI_P2an4Gl_QI
VGxbUAR1gIA-pEAAYASAAEgKb8_D_BwE.